Developing Network Organizations

Organizations

Learning from Practice and Theory

Rupert F. Chisholm
Pennsylvania State University Harrisburg

 **ADDISON-WESLEY**

An imprint of Addison Wesley Longman, Inc.

Reading, Massachusetts • Menlo Park, California • New York • Harlow, England
Don Mills, Ontario • Sydney • Mexico City • Madrid • Amsterdam

Library of Congress Cataloging-in-Publication Data

Chisholm, Rupert F.
   Developing network organizations : learning from practice and theory /
Rupert F. Chisholm.
      p.   cm. -- (Addison-Wesley series on organizational development)
      Includes bibliographical references (p.) and index.
      ISBN 0-201-87444-X
      1. Business networks. 2. Business networks--Case studies.
   3. Community networks. 4. Community networks—Case studies.
   I. Title. II. Series: Addison-Wesley series on organization development.
   HD69.S8C45 1998
   302.3'5—dc21   97-18089
                                                                       CIP

This book is in the Addison-Wesley Series on Organizational Development.
Editors: Edgar H. Schein, Richard Beckhard

ISBN 0-201-87444-X
1 2 3 4 5 6 7 8 9 10-BAM–00999897

To Virginia, Ann, Laura, Allan, and Alex

Other Titles in the
Organizational Development Series

Organizational Learning II: Theory, Method, and Practice
Chris Argyris and Donald A. Schön
1996 (0-201-62983-6)
This text addresses how business firms, governments, non-governmental organizations, schools, health care systems, regions, and whole nations need to adapt to changing environments, draw lessons from past successes and failures, detect and correct the errors of the past, anticipate and respond to impending threats, conduct experiments, engage in continuing innovation, and build and realize images of a desirable future. There is a virtual consensus that we are all subject to a "learning imperative," and in the academy no less than in the world of practice, organizational learning has become an idea in good currency.

Integrated Strategic Change: How OD Builds Competitive Advantage
Christopher G. Worley, David E. Hitchin, and Walter L. Ross
1996 (0-201-85777-4)
This book is about strategic change and how firms can improve their performance and effectiveness. Its unique contribution is in describing how organization development practitioners can assist in the effort. Strategic change is a type of organization change that realigns an organization's strategy, structure and process within a given competitive context. It is substantive and systemic and therefore differs from traditional organization development that produces incremental improvements, addresses only one system at a time, or does not intend to increase firm-level performance.

Team Building: Current Issues and New Alternatives, Third Edition
William G. Dyer
1995 (0-201-62882-1)
One of the major developments in the field of organization redesign has been the emergence of self-directed work teams. This book explains how teams are most successful when the team becomes part of the culture and structure or systems of the organization. It discusses the major new trends and emphasizes the degree of commitment that managers and members must bring to the team-building process. It is written for managers and human resource professionals who want to develop a more systematic program of team building in their organization or work unit.

Creating Labor-Management Partnerships
Warner P. Woodworth and Christopher B. Meek
1995 (0-201-58823-4)
This book begins with a call for changing the social and political barriers existing in unionized work settings and emphasizes the critical need for union-management cooperation in the present context of international competition. It demonstrates the shift from confrontational union-management relationships toward more effective and positive systems of collaboration. It is written for human resource management and industrial relations managers and staff, union officials, professional arbitrators and mediators, government officials, and professors and students involved in the study of organization development.

Organization Development: A Process of Learning and Changing,
Second Edition
W. Warner Burke
1994 (0-201-50835-4)
This text provides a comprehensive overview of the field of organization development. Written for managers, executives, administrators, practitioners, and students, this book takes an in-depth look at organization development with particular emphasis on the importance of learning and change. The author not only describes the basic tenets of OD, but he also looks at OD as a change in an organization's culture. Frameworks and models like the Burke-Litwin model (Chapter 7), as well as numerous case examples, are used throughout the book to enhance the reader's understanding of the principles and practices involved in leading and managing organizational change.

Competing with Flexible Lateral Organizations, Second Edition
Jay R. Galbraith
1994 (0-201-50836-2)
This book focuses on creating competitive advantage by building a lateral capability, thereby enabling a firm to respond flexibly in an uncertain world. The book addresses international coordination and cross-business coordination as well as the usual cross-functional efforts. It is unique in covering both cross-functional (lateral or horizontal) coordination, as well as international and corporate issues.

The Dynamics of Organizational Levels: A Change Framework for
Managers and Consultants
Nicholas S. Rashford and David Coghlan
1994 (0-201-54323-0)
This book introduces the idea that, for successful change to occur, organizational interventions have to be coordinated across the major levels of issues that all organizations face. Individual level, team level, inter-unit level, and

organizational level issues are identified and analyzed, and the kinds of intervention appropriate to each level are spelled out.

Total Quality: A User's Guide for Implementation
Dan Ciampa
1992 (0-201-54992-1)
This is a book that directly addresses the challenge of how to make Total Quality work in a practical, no-nonsense way. The companies that will dominate markets in the future will be those that deliver high quality, competitively priced products and service just when the customer wants them and in a way that exceeds the customer's expectations. The vehicle by which these companies move to that stage is Total Quality.

Becoming a Learning Organization: Beyond the Learning Curve
Joop Swieringa and André Wierdsma
1992 (0-201-62753-1)
As organizations evolve with time, the ability to learn and change is becoming increasingly more difficult. The future poses numerous obstacles and challenges for all organizations, and having the proper learning tools will provide a necessary competitive advantage. This text not only analyzes what a learning organization is, but it also explores practical approaches and tools that teach a company to "learn to learn." The aim of this book is to identify and define the learning process, and also to begin the implementation of it in order to gain an advantage in a highly competitive environment.

Managing in the New Team Environment: Skills, Tools, and Methods
Larry Hirschhorn
1991 (0-201-52503-8)
This text is designed to help manage the tensions and complexities that arise for managers seeking to guide employees in a team environment. Based on an interactive video course developed at IBM, the text takes managers step by step through the process of building a team and authorizing it to act while they learn to step back and delegate. Specific issues addressed include how to give a team structure, how to facilitate its basic processes, and how to acknowledge differences in relationships among team members and between the manager and individual team members.

Leading Business Teams: How Teams Can Use Technology and Group Process Tools to Enhance Performance
Robert Johansen, David Sibbett, Suzyn Benson, Alexia Martin,
Robert Mittman, and Paul Saffo
1991 (0-201-52829-0)
What technology or tools should organization development people or team leaders have at their command, now and in the future? This text explores the intersection of technology and business teams, a new and largely uncharted

area that goes by several labels, including "groupware"—a term that encompasses both electronic and nonelectronic tools for teams. This is the first book of its kind from the field describing what works for business teams and what does not.

The Conflict-Positive Organization: Stimulate Diversity and Create Unity
Dean Tjosvold
1991 (0-201-51485-0)
This book describes how managers and employees can use conflict to find common ground, solve problems, and strengthen morale and relationships. By showing how well-managed conflict invigorates and empowers teams and organizations, the text demonstrates how conflict is vital for a company's continuous improvement and increased competitive advantage.

Change by Design
Robert R. Blake, Jane Srygley Mouton, and Anne Adams McCanse
1989 (0-201-50748-X)
This book develops a systematic approach to organization development and provides readers with rich illustrations of coherent planned change. The book involves testing, examining, revising, and strengthening conceptual foundations in order to create sharper corporate focus and increased predictability of successful organization development.

Self-Designing Organizations: Learning How to Create
High Performance
Susan Albers Mohrman and Thomas G. Cummings
1989 (0-201-14603-7)
This book looks beyond traditional approaches to organizational transition, offering a strategy for developing organizations that enables them to learn not only how to adjust to the dynamic environment in which they exist, but also how to achieve a higher level of performance. This strategy assumes that change is a learning process: the goal is continually refined as organizational members learn how to function more effectively and respond to dynamic conditions in their environment.

Power and Organization Development: Mobilizing Power to
Implement Change
Larry E. Greiner and Virginia E. Schein
1988 (0-201-12185-9)
This book forges an important collaborative approach between two opposing and often contradictory approaches to management: OD practitioners who espouse a "more humane" workplace without understanding the political realities of getting things done, and practicing managers who feel com-

fortable with power but overlook the role of human potential in contributing to positive results.

Designing Organizations for High Performance
David P. Hanna
1988 (0-201-12693-1)
This book is the first to give insight into the actual processes you can use to translate organizational concepts into bottom-line improvements. Hanna's "how-to" approach shows not only the successful methods of intervention, but also the plans behind them and the corresponding results.

Process Consultation, Volume 1: Its Role in Organization Development, Second Edition
Edgar H. Schein
1988 (0-201-06736-6)
How can a situation be influenced in the workplace without the direct use of power or formal authority? This book presents the core theoretical foundations and basic prescriptions for effective management.

Organizational Transitions: Managing Complex Change, Second Edition
Richard Beckhard and Reuben T. Harris
1987 (0-201-10887-9)
This book discusses the choices involved in developing a management system appropriate to the "transition state." It also discusses commitment to change, organizational culture, and increasing and maintaining productivity, creativity, and innovation.

Stream Analysis: A Powerful Way to Diagnose and Manage Organizational Change
Jerry I. Porras
1987 (0-201-05693-3)
Drawing on a conceptual framework that helps the reader to better understand organizations, this book shows how to diagnose failings in organizational functioning and how to plan a comprehensive set of actions needed to change the organization into a more effective system.

Process Consultation, Volume II: Lessons for Managers and Consultants
Edgar H. Schein
1987 (0-201-06744-7)
This book shows the viability of the process consultation model for working with human systems. Like Schein's first volume on process consultation, the second volume focuses on the moment-to-moment behavior of the manager or consultant rather than the design of the OD program.

Managing Conflict: Interpersonal Dialogue and Third-Party Roles,
Second Edition
Richard E. Walton
1987 (0-201-08859-2)
This book shows how to implement a dialogue approach to conflict management. It presents a framework for diagnosing recurring conflicts and suggests several basic options for controlling or resolving them.

Pay and Organization Development
Edward E. Lawler
1981 (0-201-03990-7)
This book examines the important role that reward systems play in organization development efforts. By combining examples and specific recommendations with conceptual material, it organizes the various topics and puts them into a total systems perspective. Specific pay approaches such as gainsharing, skill-based pay, and flexible benefits are discussed, and their impact on productivity and the quality of work life is analyzed.

Work Redesign
J. Richard Hackman and Greg R. Oldham
1980 (0-201-02779-8)
This book is a comprehensive, clearly written study of work design as a strategy for personal and organizational change. Linking theory and practical technologies, it develops traditional and alternative approaches to work design that can benefit both individuals and organizations.

Organizational Dynamics: Diagnosis and Intervention
John P. Kotter
1978 (0-201-03890-0)
This book offers managers and OD specialists a powerful method of diagnosing organizational problems and of deciding when, where, and how to use (or not use) the diverse and growing number of organizational improvement tools that are available today. Comprehensive and fully integrated, the book includes many different concepts, research findings, and competing philosophies and provides specific examples of how to use the information to improve organizational functioning.

Career Dynamics: Matching Individual and Organizational Needs
Edgar H. Schein
1978 (0-201-06834-6)
This book studies the complexities of career development from both an individual and an organizational perspective. Changing needs throughout the adult life cycle, interaction of work and family, and integration of individual and organizational goals through human resource planning and development are all thoroughly explored.

Matrix
Stanley M. Davis and Paul Lawrence
1977 (0-201-01115-8)
This book defines and describes the matrix organization, a significant departure from the traditional "one man-one boss" management system. The authors note that the tension between the need for independence (fostering innovation) and order (fostering efficiency) drives organizations to consider a matrix system. Among the issues addressed are reasons for using a matrix, methods for establishing one, the impact of the system on individuals, its hazards, and what types of organizations can use a matrix system.

Feedback and Organization Development: Using Data-Based Methods
David A. Nadler
1977 (0-201-05006-4)
This book addresses the use of data as a tool for organizational change. It attempts to bring together some of what is known from experience and research and to translate that knowledge into useful insights for those who are thinking about using data-based methods in organizations. The broad approach of the text is to treat a whole range of questions and issues considering the various uses of data as an organizational change tool.

Organization Development: Strategies and Models
Richard Beckhard
1969 (0-201-00448-8)
This book is written for managers, specialists, and students of management who are concerned with the planning of organization development programs to resolve the dilemmas brought about by a rapidly changing environment. Practiced teams of interdependent people must spend real time improving their methods of working, decision making, and communicating, and a planned, managed change is the first step toward effecting and maintaining these improvements.

Series Foreword

The Addison-Wesley Series on Organizational Development originated in the late 1960s when a number of us recognized that the
rapidly growing field of "OD" was not well understood or well defined. We also recognized that there was no one OD philosophy;
hence, one could not at that time write a textbook on the theory and
practice of OD, but one could make clear what various practitioners
were doing under that label. So the original six books in the OD
Series launched what became a continuing enterprise, the essence of
which was to allow different authors to speak for themselves rather
than to summarize under one umbrella what was obviously a rapidly
growing and highly diverse field.

By the early 1980s, OD was growing by leaps and bounds and
expanding into all kinds of organizational areas and technologies of
intervention. By this time, many textbooks existed that tried to capture core concepts in the field, but we felt that diversity and innovation continued to be the more salient aspects of OD. Accordingly, our
series had expanded to nineteen titles.

As we moved into the 1990s, we began to see some real convergence in the underlying assumptions of OD. As we observed how
different professionals working in different kinds of organizations
and occupational communities made their cases, we saw that we
were still far from having a single "theory" of organizational development. Yet, some common premises were surfacing. We began to
see patterns in what was working and what was not, and we were becoming more articulate about these patterns. We also started to view

the field of OD as increasingly connected to other organizational sciences and disciplines, such as information technology, coordination theory, and organization theory.

In the early 90s, we added several new titles to the OD Series to describe important new themes: Ciampa's *Total Quality* illustrates the important link to employee involvement in continuous improvement; Johansen et. al.'s *Leading Business Teams* explores the important arena of electronic information tools for teamwork; Tjosvold's *The Conflict-Positive Organization* shows how conflict management can turn conflict into constructive action; and Hirschhorn's *Managing in the New Team Environment* builds bridges to group psychodynamic theory.

In the mid 1990s, we continued to explore emerging themes with four revisions and three new books. Burke took his highly successful *Organization Development* into new realms with more current and expanded content; Galbraith updated and enlarged his classic theory of how information management lies at the heart of organization design with his new edition of *Competing with Flexible Lateral Organizations*; and Dyer wrote an important third edition of his classic book on *Team Building*. In addition, Rashford and Coghlan introduced the important concept of levels of organizational complexity as a basis for intervention theory in their book *The Dynamics of Organizational Levels*; in *Creating Labor-Management Partnerships*, Woodworth and Meek take us into the critical realm of how OD can help in labor relations—an area that has become increasingly important as productivity issues become critical for global competitiveness; In *Integrated Strategic Change*, authors Worley, Hitchin and Ross powerfully demonstrate how the field of OD must be linked to the field of strategy by reviewing the role of OD at each stage of the strategy planning and implementation process; and finally, authors Argyris and Schön provided an important link to organizational learning in a new version of their classic book entitled *Organizational Learning II: Theory, Method, and Practice*.

Now, as we continue to think about the field of OD and what it will mean in the twenty-first century, we have added Rupert Chisholm's book, *Developing Network Organizations: Learning from Practice and Theory*, to the series. This important text explores and illustrates the link between OD and building community networks.

Our series on Organizational Development now includes over thirty titles. We will continue to welcome new titles and revisions as we explore the various frontiers of organization development and identify themes that are relevant to the ever more difficult problem of helping organizations to remain effective in an increasingly turbulent environment.

New York, New York Richard H. Beckhard
Cambridge, Massachusetts Edgar H. Schein

Foreword

It is probably an understatement to say that we live in a network society, where people, organizations, and nations are joined together by complex webs of relationships. Rapid advances in science, technology, and culture have enormously compressed time, space, and social distance, thus making the planet smaller and its inhabitants more tightly bound together. This connectedness has spawned myriad networks, some formal and informal, some involving direct and indirect relationships. Because networks are the medium through which we exchange information, resources, and influence with each other, they have momentous consequences on our lives. They enable us to transcend individual limitations by joining with others to solve common problems and to develop useful innovations. Conversely, networks make us more vulnerable to intended and unintended actions of others; they can amplify, distort, and accelerate the consequences of our interactions, thus making the world far more uncertain and dangerous.

Perhaps nowhere are linkages more prevalent than among organizations, where over the past decade, we have witnessed unprecedented growth in network forms of organizing. Business firms have increasingly turned to network strategies for teaming up with other companies to share information and resources and to benefit mutually from each others' competence. They have formed strategic alliances, joint ventures, consortia, and other types of multiorganization networks to gain access to new technologies and markets, to share risks of costly research and innovation, and to coordinate exchanges and services to drive down transaction costs. In the public sector, government agencies also are pioneering new ways of linking with each other. Faced with scarce resources, complicated problems, and demands for greater service, public organizations are increasingly joining together to eliminate costly duplication of services, to gain economies of scale, and to resolve problems that are too complex and multifaceted to tackle alone. New forms of organization are even occurring across the public and private sectors—revitalizing communities and responding to shared problems in health care, education, family life, the natural environment, and the economy.

Despite the proliferation of networks, this new form of organizing faces unique problems that are not easily resolved. Organizations traditionally look inward to resolve their problems, and thus may not consider building networks with other organizations. They may fear losing autonomy and resources to potential partners. Motivation to link may be low or absent. Organizations may not perceive the benefit of building networks or may judge costs as outweighing gains. They may encounter political, cultural, and economic barriers to such organizing, such as antitrust laws, individualistic values, and unstable economies. Even when organizations perceive the need and are motivated to develop new network forms, they may not be able to identify and attract suitable partners with similar interests and motivation. Moreover, they may not have the skills and expertise to organize and manage networks of organizations, which tend to be loosely structured, nonhierarchically controlled, and difficult to sustain.

Considering the growing importance of multiorganization networks and the problems associated with them, heavy investments are being made to find effective solutions. At the societal level, government and industry are increasingly seeking ways to create a better climate for such organizing. In the United States, this has resulted in new legislation and economic incentives to promote networks among firms, particularly in industries that have been hard hit by foreign competition. Scholars and practitioners are developing methods to help organizations resolve the organizing and managing problems of networks. This has resulted in an emerging field of planned change aimed at networks of organizations rather than single organizations. Based on the early work of Eric Trist and his colleagues, this new practice helps organizations discover the need to develop networks, to identify appropriate partners, and to organize them for joint performance. It has led to new organizing principles and change practices for creating and developing network organizations.

Rupert Chisholm's book is a significant contribution to this emerging field of planned change. It defines clearly the nature and consequences of network organizations and the environmental conditions that give rise to them. The book does an excellent job of integrating relevant concepts with appropriate methods and practices. It presents this material in the context of rich case studies filled with thick descriptions of what it is like to develop network organizations. Chisholm brings us along on his highly personal and engaging journey of learning about and helping network organizations. What makes this book all the more impressive is the rigorous and comprehensive analysis that Chisholm offers throughout. He pulls no punches and shows us both the rewards and the difficulties of doing this form of planned change. Chisholm presents a balanced account of the network development process, going beyond his own perceptions to include those of the participants themselves. Unlike so much of the popular literature on organization improvement today, this book presents no quick fixes or lists of success factors. It provides a realistic appraisal of how to develop network organizations. The book reminds me of some of the early classics on planned change from such pioneers as Warren Bennis, Ed Schein, Stan Seashore, Herb Shepard, and Eric Trist. You cannot ask for better company.

University of Southern California   Thomas G. Cummings

Preface

A network is a set of autonomous organizations that come together to reach goals that none of them can reach separately It represents a comparatively new and increasingly important form of organization—one that reflects the environmental conditions in which organizations operate. These conditions include the growing complexity of key problems or issues, the increasing interdependence among organizations and institutions, and the accelerating pace of change.

Ackoff (1974) points out that many important current problems are "messes" that actually involve sets of interconnected problems. Examples of such sets of problems are community or regional economic development efforts and attempts to reform public education to meet global competitive standards. The multifaceted nature of these problems makes them extremely difficult to conceptualize and analyze and thus immune to simple solutions. A solution to one aspect of the problem that fails to account for the possible effects of that solution on other interconnected organizations usually fails. This complexity and interdependence often require extensive collaboration among different types and various levels of organizations—public, private, labor, management, and local, state, and federal government. Adding to the complexity are existing organizational boundaries, budget and control systems, and pre-conceived perceptions and attitudes about other organizations. These and other factors make coordinated progress toward a more desirable state very difficult. Forming and developing interorganizational networks represents a response to this complexity and interdependence. Observers, such as Alter and Hage (1993), predict that networks will become the key form of organization in the next 25 years and beyond.

Traditionally organization development (OD) has tended to focus on the work group or department, work site (e.g., a plant), or total organization in relatively well-bounded systems. Rarely has it focused on attempts to develop loosely linked systems consisting of diverse groups, organizations and institutions required to deal with complex meta problems or issues. Exceptions include Trist's (1986) work in assisting the socioeconomic development of Jamestown, New York; Gricar and Brown's (1981) help in reversing housing discrimination in an urban community; and Brown's (1993) ongoing work with developing non-governmental organizations (NGOs) in third-world countries. The growing number of complex problems and issues that require interorganizational collaboration calls for fresh consideration of the network as the target of future work on system development. Attention to how networks are developed is needed so that sets of interrelated organizations within larger contexts, such as communities and regions, can make progress on solving key meta problems and issues.

Several factors prompted me to write this book. First, fieldwork, reading, and action research during the past ten years have clearly indicated the growing importance of interorganizational networks. Second, recent work in helping develop several different interorganizational networks has demonstrated to me the power of using networks to deal with many of today's complex socioeconomic problems and issues. Interorganizational networks have the capacity to enable diverse organizations and groups to collaborate around a shared vision and purpose to bring about positive change. Due to the flexibility of these networks, this capacity exists under many different conditions—different issues or problems, different types of stakeholders, different settings. Third, direct experience has also revealed some of the complexity and difficulty involved in bringing diverse organizations and groups together to carry out a larger purpose. Hence, there is a need to invent and discover effective models, strategies, and techniques for helping networks develop. Learning from network development efforts can help here. Fourth, using action research to help these systems develop has helped me gain some understanding of the nature of networks and ways of working with them. This book attempts to share what I've learned with you.

Since network organizations are expected to be the key form of organization in coming decades, it is essential to understand more about these systems and how to develop them to meet requirements in specific situations. It is also important to help individuals and organizations learn how to collaborate to create desirable futures. Developing Network Organizations attempts to reach these goals. It is aimed at three main audiences:

1. Managers of public, private, and nonprofit organizations involved in interorganizational networks, or partnerships focused on important broad issues on problems.
2. OD/systems development professionals, consultants, and facilitators involved in creating, maintaining, and developing interorganizational networks.
3. Graduate and advanced undergraduate students of organizations/system development and change, for whom it can serve as a second reader in a general course on organization and system development.

The book is organized into five parts:

- *Part I—Introduction:* A brief description of the New Baldwin Corridor Coalition opens Chapter 1 to illustrate the definition of "interorganizational network" used in the book. A short account of leading features of the interorganizational network model follows. The chapter concludes by identifying several factors in the external general environment that are making the interorganizational network an increasingly important form of organization.

- *Part II—Developing an Industrial Community for the Twenty-first Century:* The four chapters in this part present the development of the New Baldwin Corridor Coalition. Chapter 2 describes events leading to creating the coalition, how I became involved with it, and early development work during the first year. Chapter 3 covers the evolution of sponsoring, designing, and conducting a community strategic planning conference. A substantially modified search conference design was used for this meeting. Work to prepare for, conduct, and follow through on the conference had substantial impacts on developing the coalition as a network organization. Chapter 4 traces network development during the second year of coalition existence. Key events during this period include supporting collaboration among several public school districts, two vocational schools, and two institutions of higher education, developing a set of goals and projects for the next two years, and serving as a catalyst/supporter in making several tangible outcomes happen. Chapter 5 covers important incidents in developing New Baldwin as a network organization from January 1994 to early 1997.

- *Part III—Developing a Rural Business Incubator Network:* This segment of the book describes activity designed to develop an interorganizational network among 14 widely dispersed independent local business incubators in a large region of Pennsylvania. Chapter 6 describes my getting involved in the project, building an approach for network development, linking with the system, and designing and conducting the first development conference. Chapter 7 covers later interventions and outcomes of the development process. External constraints limited work with this system to one year. The case is thus helpful because it follows the organization development process through all its phases, from initial contact through final feedback and action planning.

- *Part IV—Developing a Network of Community Organizations:* Chapter 8 describes the emergence, development, and activities of a third interorganizational network, the Inter-church Network for Social Concerns which originated in a small rural town in early 1993. Over time, the network has gained the capacity to identify, define, and develop consensus about broad community issues and to help discover ways of dealing with them. This chapter presents origins of the network, its development, and the impact of its work.

- *Part V—Learnings and Implications:* Chapter 9 identifies the learnings derived from my work in helping develop the three network organizations covered in the book. My attempt here is to convey the complexity and often conflicting dynamics of network development work. I also hope that these insights will help guide developing interorganizational networks in other settings.

    Chapter 10 covers two recent network development efforts that have special importance for the future. One case involves developing the Nordvest Forum, a large group of organizations in a remote region of Norway, into a learning network. The purpose of the network is to increase the ability of the region to compete in the international marketplace by improving the management capacity of organizations. The second case describes development of a global network to deal with lingering problems of orphans following collapse of the Romanian government in 1989. This case illustrates using network development as a way of organizing the work of various types of organizations in many different countries and focusing the effort on a complex problem in one nation.

The last chapter highlights major points covered in earlier parts of the book and draws conclusions from them about developing networks in the future.

Gettysburg, Pennsylvania   R.F.C.

Acknowledgments

Writing this book would have been impossible without the help and support of many individuals. Virginia Schein, my lovely wife, has been the most important supporter from beginning to end. Her encouragement to write the book and continuing encouragement and support during the writing process, especially during some "down times," was crucial—I couldn't have done it without her. And, at the task level, she made numerous helpful comments on the several drafts of the various chapters.

Colleagues directly involved in the projects have been a constant source of support and learning. They have provided help in figuring out what is going on, and, together, we have devised ways of developing the interorganizational networks involved. In developing the New Baldwin Corridor Coalition, Ike Gittlen has been essential as a visionary leader who saw (and sees) the "big picture." He welcomed me to the project and we have worked together along with many others for over five years to develop and maintain the coalition. My good friend and colleague, Dennis Bellafiore, has been a close "partner in crime" on New Baldwin since early 1993. We work together as an OD team. And, for the past two years, Weng Wah Tam (Tam) has provided invaluable research assistant support as part of our OD team. His contributions go well beyond those of a typical doctoral student research assistant. Thanks also go to the steering committee and several hundred other members of the coalition for their substantial pioneer work in developing a new type of organization to improve the greater community.

Gregg Lichtenstein and I worked as close colleagues on developing the Central and Northern Incubator Group as a network organization. Together we ventured into a highly ambiguous situation, figured out some ways of making sense of it, and devised interventions that helped members develop elements of a system into a network. Tam also was a key member of our action research team. Their inputs and support made development work possible and contributed greatly to learnings and enjoyment derived from the project. The local incubator managers who formed and joined the network deserve special recognition. They took time from busy, hectic work schedules to engage in development interventions when possible outcomes were far from clear. Support from the steering committee was also crucial. And, funding from the Center for Rural Pennsylvania made the development process possible.

Developing the Inter-church Network for Social Concerns has been a team effort from the beginning. The steering committee of eight persons provides leadership and coordination. Members' willingness to experiment and learn has made the network possible. But the network also extends to the churches, other community organizations, and individuals who have become involved in various network projects. Positive responses by them on several issues that the network identified have helped improve the community. Thanks go to all of these individuals and organizations for enabling me to learn with them by doing.

Support from many other colleagues who have not been directly involved in the reported cases also has contributed to the book. Tom Cummings introduced me to the social ecology thinking of Eric Trist and Fred Emery over 25 years ago. Their way of conceptualizing important higher-level issues "rang true" to me then and today provides a foundation for engaging in network development. More recently, when I was considering writing this book, Tom gave instant encouragement—"Do it! It's important and there isn't anything like that out there!" This spurred me on.

Other colleagues have helped in many different ways. In 1987 Max Elden arranged for me to spend the summer at the University of Trondheim, Norway. This opened up contacts with Norwegian and Swedish colleagues. Several deserve special mention. Thoralf Qvale and Henrik Finsrud at the Work Research Institute in Oslo have become very good friends and colleagues. Their work and that of other Norwegian colleagues, such as Jan Hanssen-Bauer, provide ongoing stimulation and input for my work. Similarly, Bjorn Gustavsen's work in Sweden and Norway provides other new ideas and a different experience base for conducting network development. In addition, Max Elden and I have become close friends and colleagues via convening and coordinating "Action Research/Empowering Work Network" workshops at the Academy of Management meeting each August for the past ten years. This has provided a continuing base of support and inputs on new network development work in many parts of the world. During the past few years, the work of Dave Cooperrider, Diana Billimoria, and Tim Wilmot on global change issues has extended my thinking about developing interorganizational networks. My sincere thanks go to these and many other unnamed colleagues for helping me learn some things about developing network organizations.

Special thanks go to Joette Swartz who typed and edited several drafts of the manuscript. Her patience, good humor, and speed contributed greatly to completing the book on time. I greatly appreciate her effort and the high quality of her work.

Professors Edgar Schein and Richard Beckhard, consulting editors for the Addison-Wesley OD Series, also played a key role in developing the book. Initially, they expressed strong support for the concept of the book and encouraged me to develop the outline into a full manuscript. Later, their feedback on the several drafts was essential in making the style suitable for the OD Series and in refining the manuscript. Thanks also go to Kate Morgan, the first associate editor, and Mike Roche, who saw publication through to completion. Ruth Berry provided able support to each of them.

The book is dedicated with love to my wife, Virginia Schein, and children, Ann, Laura, Allan, and Alex.

Contents

Part I
Introduction to Interorganizational Networks

1

The Interorganizational Network

A Glimpse at an Interorganizational Network: The New Baldwin Corridor Coalition

Ike Gittlen, president of Local 1688 of the United Steelworkers of America, had observed what was happening to the local Bethlehem Steel plant for several years. In 1991 he began to voice his concerns about the future employment prospects of union members and the future of the Steelton, Pennsylvania, community where the plant is located. Ike's article in the Harrisburg *Patriot News* sounded a call for action by various parts of the community: "Will we continue our blind allegiance to individual action...or will we now begin to act together for mutual benefit?" Later, Ike saw a chance to galvanize support around a vision and a proposed strategy for rebuilding the economy of the community. He summarized his thoughts in a brief report, "The New Baldwin Project: Creating a Twenty-first Century Manufacturing Town." Choosing the name "New Baldwin" reflected the original name of Steelton, "Village of Baldwin." This community was established in 1865 around the first integrated steel mill in America.

The New Baldwin Corridor Coalition (NBCC) has grown from Ike's vision and call for action. The coalition grew initially from a series of open community meetings that began in February 1992. Today it operates as a network of business, labor, government, education, finance, community organizations, and economic development agencies. A steering committee comprised of representatives of various stakeholder organizations coordinates and manages coalition work. Task forces and committees have been formed to work on specific issues or areas of work. NBCC has functioned for over five years, has directly involved more than 300 leaders and citizens, and has sponsored many initiatives that required interorganizational collaboration anchored in a shared vision of the future.

Vision

What makes the coalition unique is its approach and operating principles. New Baldwin is based on the following key elements:

- A steering committee represents all stakeholders; working subcommittees focus on specific issues.
- Excess land belonging to the Bethlehem Steel Plant serves as a base site for an enterprise zone to spur economic development.
- School districts and higher education spearhead a twenty-first century educational program to develop the technical/knowledge worker.
- Organized labor explores new ways of organizing and promotes leading edge work organizations.
- Government organizations reexamine roles, structures, relationships, and authority to streamline and focus government services.
- Educational, research, technology and human resource organizations focus on leading edge industrial/manufacturing ideas.
- Funding and maximum integration is provided by various organizations, groups, and institutions.

In brief, the coalition vision emphasizes the need to involve all parts of the community in inventing new ways of thinking and taking action. Beyond the individual elements, New Baldwin has attempted to transform organizations and the total community to enable them to survive and prosper in the twenty-first century. Creating and maintaining high quality, well-paying jobs has been a top priority.

Outcomes of Coalition Work

NBCC work includes specific tangible outcomes:

- Convening a community strategic planning conference attended by approximately one hundred persons.
- Establishing a free walk-in children's immunization clinic in the corridor through collaboration with two other organizations.
- Setting up a dislocated workers' center.

- Sponsoring and conducting a survey of business leaders.
- Establishing and actively supporting the work of an education committee that has fostered collaboration among seven school districts, two vocational education schools, and two higher education institutions in the area.
- Issuing a newsletter to communicate and foster NBCC activity and related social/economic development work in greater Harrisburg.
- Developing an enterprise alliance that provides support for implementing new labor-management solutions to member problems.

Several other significant broad outcomes include:

- Having the ability to bring representatives of diverse groups and organizations together to collaborate in building an industrial community for the twenty-first century.
- Developing and demonstrating the capacity to convene, design, and manage development events that can have significant effects on the larger community.
- Achieving a workable level of understanding among members about New Baldwin as an interorganizational network, its role compared with other organizations, and its organization and management.

This brief description merely highlights several aspects of New Baldwin and introduces readers to the type of interorganizational network covered by this book. A detailed account of the development and outcomes of coalition work appears in Chapters 2 through 5.

The Nature of Interorganizational Networks

The New Baldwin coalition represents one interorganizational network. Chapters 2 through 5 will cover its development and outcomes in greater detail. Chapters 6 through 8 trace the development of two other interorganizational networks: the Central and Northern Incubator Group of fourteen widely dispersed rural business incubators (Chapters 6 and 7) and the Interchurch Network for Social Concerns (Chapter 8). Interorganizational networks are assuming increasing importance in the late 1990s and the importance of them as a new form of organization will grow well into the next century. Since these systems use nontraditional designs, readers must understand the basic nature of interorganizational networks to appreciate how to develop them. This section describes several key features of these systems.

The three projects covered in Chapters 2 through 8 used Eric Trist's socio-ecological perspective of interorganizational networks to conceptualize and guide the development process (Finsrud, 1995; Trist, 1983, 1985). Figure 1.1 summarizes key features of this view of interorganizational networks.

First, interorganizational networks operate largely as abstract conceptual systems that enable members to perceive and understand large-scale problems in new ways. Developing shared understandings makes it possible for members to create ways of organizing to deal with these complex problems.

Second, networks differ from mere interorganizational relationships. Networks improve the ability of organizations to deal with ill-defined, complex problems or issues that individual members cannot handle alone. Network activity is oriented to the shared vision, purpose, and goals that bind members together. These act as superordinate goals that incorporate but go beyond the interests of individual member organizations. Forming and developing a system to achieve a shared larger purpose is the hallmark of network organizations. This orientation affects the basic worldview and all aspects of network activities.

Third, loose-coupling of members is another feature of these systems. Members represent diverse organizations that are physically dispersed and meet from time to time to conduct activities required to carry out the higher-level system purpose. Belonging to a network is voluntary with few formal organizational structures and processes that make involvement permanent. Networks also rest on a horizontal rather than a hierarchical organizing principle: one organization or member does not have a superior-subordinate relationship with another.

Fourth, network organizations are self-regulating. Members, not a centralized source of power, are responsible for developing a vision, mission, and goals and for initiating and managing work activities. Members share their understanding of issues and devise ways to relate to each other in carrying out the work necessary to bring about a shared vision of the future. This vision provides the context that orients all network activity. Retaining this orientation is critical to developing and maintaining networks.

Conceptual systems:	Member organizations consciously develop networks to help understand and deal with complex, ambiguous problems/issues ("messes").
	Primary work of networks involves devising ways for members to think about, create, plan, conduct, and evaluate collaborative activity.
System level:	Networks exist at a level above interorganizational relationships.
	Members come together to deal with complex meta-problems that require collaborative work by many organizations.
	A shared vision and common purpose orient and guide a network and its work. These ground the network at the supra-system level.
Relationships:	Members are loosely-coupled, belong to a network voluntarily, and meet as required to conduct work.
	A horizontal form of organization exists. Members are equal, with no superior-subordinate relationships among them.
Control:	Members control the network and its activities.
	Members are responsible for developing a shared understanding of a problem area.
	Members plan, initiate, and manage network activities.
Functions:	Interorganizational networks have three basic functions:
	1. Regulation: Maintaining orientation of the network to the shared vision and purpose; assuring development/maintenance of network values and appropriate ways of organizing activities
	2. Appreciation: Developing a shared understanding of changes to the network vision and purpose required to incorporate issues/trends that emerge over time.
	3. Development support: Providing professional organization development resources required to develop, maintain, and manage the network.

Figure 1.1

Key Features of the Socio-Ecological View of Interorganizational Networks

Source: From Trist, 1983, 1985

Dave Brown (1987) captures the essence of these systems with the following statements of network organizing principles:

1. Members are included because of their interest in or their ability to contribute to constructive action.
2. Members are loosely coupled and participate in system activities voluntarily.
3. Activities and decisions revolve around a broad vision or purpose and a set of general goals that incorporate the interests of the diverse organizations and individuals.

These key features of interorganizational networks form the basis of the development work described in Chapters 2 through 8. Further discussion of how these features are applied will occur in the discussion and analyses of specific cases.

Why Interorganizational Networks Are Becoming More Important

The environmental conditions of today place complex demands on organizations. Technological change, constantly expanding knowledge, globalization, and changing beliefs and values combine with other aspects of the environment to cause the turbulence faced by organizations. These complex problems defy straightforward analysis and solutions. According to Alter and Hage (1993), the interorganizational network that matches system capability with complex, rapidly changing environments will become the key form of organization in the future. This section briefly describes several factors that apply pressures to create interorganizational networks.

Technology

Fred Emery noted that computers, microprocessors, and other rapid information-processing devices comprise the lead technology of the postindustrial era (Emery, 1978). Rapidly evolving communication systems—from E-mail to the fax to the Internet—have further enhanced our ability to manipulate and transmit information instantaneously around the globe.

Computer and communications technologies thus affect the potential location and arrangement of organizational units. Manufacturing organizations no longer have to hire large numbers of employees at one location to produce products. Automobile manufacturers, for instance, can contract with subcontractors to build large components such as integrated dashboards or body panels that the final assembly plant merely "snaps" together. Insurance and financial service companies have data processing units located abroad. Increasingly, computers and rapid communications systems thus enable managers to link remote locations and integrate total work processes.

Figure 1.2 identifies several features of existing and emerging technologies that reduce the importance of physical location sig-

Computer and Communications Technology	
Feature	*Basic Impact*
Fiber optic transmission systems	Virtually cost-free connections
Cordless, cellular, and satellite phones	Increased mobility; communications to person, not place
Video conferencing	Carrying out group discussions among individuals located in many places
Video voicemail	Time compression
Telepresence	Carrying out hazardous or delicate work procedures from remote locations
In-line converters	Simultaneous translation of languages
Transportation	
Feature	*Basic Impact*
Super trains	Rapid delivery of goods and people within geographic regions
Ultrasonic aircraft	Capacity to reduce air travel time significantly
Integrated multimodal systems	Rapid delivery of goods throughout the world

Figure 1.2
Technological Factors and the Decreasing Importance of Place

Source: From Knoke, 1996, pp. 18–46.

nificantly. For example, expanding fiber optic systems will reduce the costs of transmitting information anywhere in the world to virtually zero. Video conferencing equipment will enable scientists, politicians, and businesspeople to conduct "face-to-face" discussions over great distances and personal in-line converters will provide simultaneous language translation. Overall, existing and new electronics technologies will greatly extend worldwide communication capabilities.

Transportation technologies will also contribute to the decreasing importance of place. The French network of 200-mile-per hour trains and the Japanese "bullet train" illustrate the growing use of high-speed regional ground transportation. Other countries, including the United States, plan to introduce super trains during the next 20 years. Somewhat later, ultrasonic aircraft will enable people to travel globally from point to point at astonishing speeds—from New York to Berlin in 54 minutes, to India in 79 minutes, and to Australia in 87 minutes (Sweeney and Bandon, 1996). The development of large air freight transports and the reduced weight of products through miniaturization and the use of lightweight materials will transform air cargo transportation. Integrating various modes of transportation makes it possible to transfer goods with a minimal loss of time. For example, the Port of Tacoma coordinates ocean shipping, two railroads, and approximately 200 truck lines to move cargo from point of origin to destination with minimum lost time. Combining rapid electronic processing and transmission technologies with new transportation technologies further lessens the importance of place.

In short, advanced technology is ushering in an era of "placelessness." According to Knoke (1996), a placeless society has the capacity to make virtually everything, including people, knowledge, and resources, available anywhere, often simultaneously, regardless of physical location. This capacity to link widely dispersed units around the world, coupled with global competition and rapidly changing environments, applies pressures to create interorganizational networks.

Growth of Knowledge

Advanced industrial societies around the world have entered a postindustrial era whose leading features include the increased professionalism of the workplace, the rising importance of theoretical knowledge, and the provision of services rather than goods. Daniel

Bell (1976) identifies the utilization of theoretical knowledge as the driving force of the new era.

Producing this new knowledge occurs in many ways—from research and development, high-technology production systems to organizational learning processes, workplace design, and higher levels of education. Hage and Powers (1992) point out that creating and using knowledge leads to more complex work roles.

Figure 1.3 compares the leading features of occupational roles in the industrial and postindustrial eras. For example, the industrial

	Industrial Roles (Rationalization)	**Postindustrial Roles (Complexification)**
Mechanization (technology)	Simple machines	Sophisticated instruments that yield better information for workers to act upon
Codification of rules (or emphasis on scripts, techniques, or behavior	Many specific rules and little room for human discretion	Few specific rules and great deal of room for human discretion
Routinization	Standardization of procedures and little need for information search	Emphasis on customized response and great need for information search
Skills/training	Reduction of the number of roles, and deskilling of remaining roles	Proliferation of specialized fields and upgrading of skill levels required for most roles
Primary performance criteria	Efficiency and quantity, or large volume	Innovation, quality, customization, and personalized service

Figure 1.3
Aspects of Occupational Roles in Industrial and Postindustrial Eras

Source: Hage and Powers, 1992, p. 51. Reprinted by permission of Sage Publications, Inc.

age emphasized rationalization, which typically led to simplifying jobs and work procedures following the principles of scientific management. Rationalization rested on a machine model of organization and work processes, and it involved using relatively simple machines, adopting rules that dictated many aspects of workers' behavior, specifying work procedures in detail, and emphasizing system efficiency and quantity of production. The postindustrial era emphasizes complexification, which has led to the use of more complex machines that combine with complex work processes that require workers to use information and knowledge to make decisions. In short, with fewer rules prescribing behavior the amount of discretion inherent in jobs is increasing. Primary performance criteria of quality and customized products or services require that workers search for and invent solutions. Providing the quality and tailored responses required fosters a general upgrading of knowledge and skills and development of many specialized fields. Overall, the growing importance of knowledge in the workplace requires inventing new organizational designs. The interorganizational network is a leading form of organization that helps meet increasing requirements to use and generate knowledge.

Globalization
Another feature of postindustrialism is the rising importance of relationships among nations participating in the global economy and the changes generated in various political and economic institutions. For example, as traditional nation-states decline in relative importance, transfers of responsibilities will occur, with some functions shifting to international organizations and others to subnational levels. Economic institutions also change, showing a corresponding shift to multilevel arrangements. Commenting on these changes, Perlmutter and Trist (1986) state that, "For some commodities, trade would continue on a world basis; for others it would be regional; for others again, it would be local, where self-reliance would be appropriate." Changes will reflect attempts to adapt organizations and institutions to the increasing complexity and turbulence of the environment. Various types of interorganizational networks will be created in response to these conditions.

Recent work by Rosabeth Moss Kanter (1995) fills in details of several changes noted above. She asserts that the century of American and European dominance of the world economy is passing rapidly. In its place, a global century has begun. Having the capacity to be "world class" is the basic requirement for participating successfully in the new age. And reaching and maintaining world class status requires three types of intangible assets:

1. Concepts: the best and latest knowledge and ideas.
2. Competence: the ability to meet the highest operating standards that exist anywhere in the world.
3. Connections: effective linkages to individuals, organizations, and institutions around the globe.

Having a cosmopolitan perspective is also essential for organizations to develop the capacity to function effectively today.

Many conflicting pressures will face managers and leaders in the new era. For example, business managers must be strongly rooted in communities while also being connected to wider networks throughout the world. Politicians and public managers will need similar linkages. In addition, since regional economies will assume greater importance in the global economy, private and public managers will find it necessary to align activities with forces from various levels—local, regional, national, international. Success under these circumstances will require collaboration, not singular activity. It will also require flexibility and the capacity to change organizations rapidly. Interorganizational networks have the capability of enabling managers to meet many of the complex, conflicting requirements of globalization.

Beliefs and Values

A basic shift in beliefs and values is emerging as part of the postindustrial transition. The emphasis on "quality of work life" programs in the early 1970s was an early indicator of this change. Despite short-run counter forces such as downsizing, gradual change to these new values is continuing. Perlmutter and Trist (1986) wrote that industrialism is starting to demonstrate through its dysfunctional outcomes that it is approaching its limits. Hence, a new set of values is required.

Several global trends are contributing to the need for a new set of beliefs (Laszlo, 1994). For example, rapid population growth poses a serious threat to the carrying capacity of the earth, while uneven population increases between industrialized and nonindustrialized countries make the problem worse. Each year approximately 95 million people are added to the world population; only 7 million are born in industrialized nations. At the same time, by some measures the world capacity to produce food is declining. Deforestation, changing weather patterns, and energy production represent other basic threats to the planet.

Technical solutions to such world problems do not exist. In fact, the set of beliefs about the nature of the world, including faith in "technological fixes," that were reasonable and productive in the industrial era, have led to the present situation. Consequently, a new set of basic beliefs about how things work must be formulated.

Figure 1.4 compares the key features of the dominant industrial view and the new age described by Laszlo (1994). Two general comments may clarify the required shifts. First, the industrial (atomistic) view of the external world is based on the law of the jungle (looking out only for oneself) and a belief in the "invisible hand," the self-regulating system of classical economics. In contrast, the postindustrial view stresses cooperation in social systems: Individuals, groups, organizations, and nations must work together for the good of the whole.

Second, the industrial view rests on a machine model of organizations and social systems: Each component is analyzed on its own with little concern about how it fits into the total system. In contrast, the postindustrial view focuses on the emerging holistic nature of organizations and higher-level social systems. Total system design principles and concepts are emphasized as are interactions among components.

Although it seems obvious that the industrial age is passing, its values and beliefs continue to guide most economic, social, and political organizations. What beliefs will enable humankind to deal effectively with many large problems and to create a desirable future? The new beliefs of the postindustrial era clearly emphasize increased interaction among growing numbers of groups, organizations, and societies. Interorganizational networks will provide a primary way of fostering new beliefs and putting them into practice.

The Nature of Current Problems

Many current socioeconomic problems are complex and share several important characteristics. Examples of national problems include fostering economic and social development in various regions, developing effective training and transition support for displaced workers, welfare reform, and developing ways of cleaning up the nation's rivers and streams. Global dilemmas include environmental degradation, increasing numbers of marginalized people, and chronic hunger

	Industrial View	**Postindustrial View**
External world	Atomistic, fragmented; objects are independent and freestanding; people are individuated and discrete	Objects and people interwoven into community
Physical processes	Materialistic, deterministic, mechanistic	Organic, interactive, holistic
Organic function	Discrete and separable; exchangeable parts	Interwoven, interdependent; not interchangeable or exchangeable
Social ethos	Technology-oriented, interventionist, goods-based	Communication-oriented, service-based
Social progress	Consumption-dependent resource conversion	Adaptation-oriented, balance of resources
Economics	Competition and profit-driven, exploitative	Cooperative and information-driven
Human role	Mastery over nature	Integration with nature
Culture	Eurocentric, colonial	Pluralistic
Politics	Hierarchical, power-based	Holarchic, harmony-based

Figure 1.4
Changing Beliefs : From the Industrial to the Postindustrial Age

Source: Laszlo, 1994, p. 6. Reprinted by permission of Gordon and Breach Publishers.

and poverty. Authors use various names for such problems. Trist (1983), for example, calls them problem domains, while Ackoff (1974) uses the term "messes." Despite the different labels, these problems have several common features:

1. Problems are "messes" and involve sets of interconnected problems. The multiple linkages and multifaceted nature of these problems make them impossible to solve by simple solutions: A solution to one aspect of the problem that fails to account for impacts on other organizations and groups that are interconnected usually fails. The complex, inter-linked character of these problems also make them extremely difficult to conceptualize, analyze, and solve.

2. Interorganization action is required. Complexity and interdependence also require that many different organizations become involved in planning and implementing ways of improving the situation. Concrete, absolute solutions are normally impossible for such large-scale problems; only gradual progress toward a more desirable state is possible. Working toward a more desirable future requires the coordinated efforts of many organizations. Absence of coordinated efforts to improve the situation frequently causes the action of one organization to create problems for others.

3. Multiple sector and organizational levels are involved. Often, the need to involve organizations from different sectors (e.g., public, private, labor, higher education) and from different levels (e.g., federal, state, local government) adds to the complexity of dealing with large-scale socioeconomic problems. For example, attempting to develop support, training, and job search assistance for former welfare recipients or displaced workers requires involvement of many organizations at the local level (e.g., company, union, social service agencies), state level (e.g., unemployment compensation, training, economic development), and federal level (e.g., Job Training Partnership Act, industrial adjustment assistance). Existing organizational boundaries, budget and control systems, and preconceived views and feelings about other organizations typically make coordinated action difficult. And this difficulty grows when organizations from different sectors are involved (e.g., a business person's perception: "Those do-gooders from social service agencies don't understand the bottom line").

Superimposing requirements from the state and federal levels often compounds the difficulty.

4. Multiple outcomes must be considered. Policy decisions and actions to deal with complex socioeconomic problems often lead to a variety of outcomes over time. Some of these will be "positive," from the viewpoint of society, others will be negative. In addition, although some of the outcomes can be predicted, others cannot. Herbst (1976) points out that often, in complex, interactive systems, planned activities that aim at desirable goals often cause unintended, undesirable outcomes. In short, outcomes of policies, programs, and planned actions are nondeterministic. For this reason, attempts to deal with messes or problem domains must incorporate the capacity to monitor outcomes constantly. On-line monitoring is needed to make rapid changes in activities in order to move the network in a positive direction.

The EPA's current initiative to encourage sustainable community development illustrates the complexity and intractability of many "messes" we currently face. The basic interdependence among environmental quality, economic prosperity, and community well-being is widely recognized. Hence, sustainable development emphasizes extensive participation of community stakeholders (e.g., government, business, community groups, labor unions) in developing ways of reaching these broad goals. While this systemic approach makes sense, the organizational, political, and technical challenges to achieving sustainable development in specific communities are daunting.

The broad, multifaceted nature of key problems such as sustainable development and the limitations of existing attempts to deal with them indicate a need to develop new approaches. One approach to solving complex socioeconomic problems is interorganizational network development. This approach rests upon experience and research on developing networks as complex, ever-changing systems designed to help multiple parties deal with complex common issues.

Conclusions

Conditions in the environment are exerting pressures that are leading to the creation of new organizational forms. The interorganizational network has emerged as the leading type of system to match requirements of environments in an increasing number of situations.

Several general features characterize the environments in which organizations operate: strong international competition, rapid and pervasive technological change, rising expectations for involvement in work decisions among the best educated groups of employees, and ever-increasing demands for high-quality products and services coupled with pressures to control costs. The growing importance of knowledge combined with the increased possibilities that leading-edge computers, information processing, and communications equipment also generate additional stimuli for change. The design and development of work systems and organizations that foster and support knowledge generation are also expanding.

A new set of postindustrial beliefs and values reinforces other pressures to develop new organizational forms. For example, our newly interdependent world raises serious questions about the efficacy of traditional bureaucratic organizations. Such questions also encourage individuals to look at outcomes beyond immediate organizational boundaries. Newer technologies that foster "placelessness" have led to the globalization of commerce and of information and knowledge dissemination. These forces have in turn encouraged lateral linkages through network organizations and weakened the viability of centralized control. The postindustrial organization must face complex problems or "messes" that defy simple solutions and require the concerted actions of a set of organizations often from different sectors and levels. The interorganizational network represents the key type of system to meet postindustrial environmental requirements.

Unfortunately, we know relatively little about the nature of interorganizational networks, how they work, and how to develop and manage them. This book represents an early attempt to fill in some of the blanks, with a heavy emphasis on ways of developing network organizations.

Part II

Developing an Industrial Community for the Twenty-First Century

2

Starting the New Baldwin Corridor Coalition

A Trip to the Belgrade Bakery

On a Friday morning in 1992, before going to the Penn State Harrisburg campus, I drove down Front Street toward the Belgrade Bakery in Steelton, Pennsylvania. An earlier visit to a local wine shop had already provided Hungarian wine for a goulash dinner with friends that evening and loaves of Yugoslav bread from the Belgrade promised to round out the meal. As the trip through Steelton continued, I began to observe the town in a new light. Since coming to the area almost twenty years ago, I had made many previous trips through Steelton—all of them depressing. The rusting hulk of a once large steel mill along the route dominated the area for over a mile. And signs of deteriorating homes and businesses were everywhere. Consequently, I avoided the route whenever possible.

The trip on this particular morning was however quite different. Maybe it was having had the good fortune to find good Hungarian wine that put me in a new frame of mind or maybe I was more relaxed anticipating spring break the next week. Whatever the reasons, I began to see Steelton in a very different light. Names like "St. Aloysius Hall," "Baldwin Fire Company #4," "St. Lawrence Club," and "Napoli Restaurant" stuck out, came alive, and communicated some of the rich long history and ethnic diversity of the town. That morning, for the first time, I saw not only an aging industrial community that had been slowly dying for years, but also the possibility of revival. My reaction was something like "What a shame! Here's a town that is being discarded as dead. There must be ways of revitalizing the community and many others like it across America. What could be done to make this happen?"

The next Tuesday, when I went into the office to check the mail, this experience came back to haunt me. A short memorandum from Bob, the associate provost for outreach, to all members of Penn State Harrisburg briefly described a new coalition of organizations that had formed to develop Steelton into a model twenty-first century community. I immediately phoned Bob to determine whether the coalition was real or merely PR fluff. Based on this conversation, it seemed worthwhile to get additional information directly from Ike Gittlen, leader of the coalition and president of the steelworkers' local that represents employees at the Bethlehem Steel Plant in Steelton. So, I phoned Ike and we made an appointment to meet in his office later in the week.

Before the meeting, Ike checked me out with several union members. Fortunately, my work several years earlier with a few union and management leaders had been positive, so the word came back that "Rupe is OK." During the meeting, Ike described the coalition; he also asked about my experience, background, and interest in becoming involved. Although I had some general ideas about possibly using action research to foster development, it was far from clear exactly how I might link into the coalition and help it develop. But I felt confident that more ideas and useful concepts would emerge after becoming involved. At the end of our meeting, Ike invited me to the next general coalition meeting. A week later at that meeting, he asked me to chair a committee and become a steering committee member. I have been actively involved in coalition work since then. It has proven to be one of the most interesting learning experiences of my career.

Creating the Coalition

A brief description of the New Baldwin Corridor Coalition opened the first chapter. Remaining sections of Chapter 2 contain more detail about the history and first year of development of the Coalition as an interorgánizational network. Coverage includes how I became involved, key events in creating New Baldwin, two planned interventions to develop the network, and several observations on this early work.

Recognizing the Problem

In late 1991, long-rumored talk of the restructuring of Bethlehem Steel Corporation grew. The threat that this posed to jobs and future operations at the Bethlehem plant in the Steelton, Pennsylvania, plant caused Ike Gittlen, the local steelworkers union president, to reflect on the situation that had emerged over several years and to pull his thoughts together. Ike's article in the Harrisburg *Patriot-News* expressed these thoughts and called for action by various parts of the community. The basic message was: "Will we continue our blind allegiance to individual action...even when it results in our own economic suicide...or will we now begin to act together for mutual benefit?" This message, which was the first public expression of the need for joint action by various groups and organizations, received favorable response from several prominent community members.

Details of the Bethlehem Steel plans emerged a short time later. On January 29, 1992, the Corporation announced a general restructuring plan to reduce costs and make the organization profitable. This plan included closing part of the Steelton plant with a loss of 400 jobs. The future of the remaining 1600 jobs remained uncertain despite mention of possible plant modernization. Ike Gittlen responded to this development by calling a news conference with county commissioners, a state senator, and a member of Congress. During the news conference, Gittlen sketched a picture of government and community leaders forming a coalition to save the immediately threatened jobs and stabilize the entire Steelton plant. Within the next week, he conducted a second news conference with a broader set of participants, including a U.S. senator, ten local, state, and federal government officials, and representatives of business and economic development organizations. A local newspaper reported that a growing sense of movement that transcended the immediate crisis began to emerge during this news conference. Together, this series of events highlighted and focused attention on the Steelton situation and suggested broader implications for the future of the community. Broad outlines of an approach for transforming the community also began to emerge from these meetings.

Creating a Vision for the Future

Based on earlier meetings, discussions, and observations, Ike Gittlen saw an opportunity to galvanize community support around a vision and a proposed strategy for dealing with basic causes of industrial decline. He summarized these thoughts in a brief report, "The New Baldwin Project: Creating a Twenty-first Century Manufacturing Town." The prologue to the report captures his vision:

> On September 22, 1865 (while the embers of the Civil War were still burning), a group of businessmen met in Philadelphia, Pennsylvania, to plan an enterprise that would become one of the bedrocks of the American Industrial Revolution. Their work resulted in the formation of the Pennsylvania Steel Company, the establishment of the

Village of Baldwin, Pennsylvania (later renamed Steelton), the erection of the first integrated steel plant in the United States, and most importantly the first plant to produce steel rails in this nation. These men, meeting at one of the bleakest times in American history, had the vision to finance and create an entirely new industrial town whose products and purpose endured for over 100 years.

Today, Steelton is a dying relic of that bygone era. Rocked by foreign competition, lack of investment in new equipment, inadequate research and development, and a failure to adopt visionary strategic planning, the plant around which it is centered no longer has the ability to sustain the town. Abandoned by the changing lifestyles of its more mobile and wealthier children, the citizenry is by and large an older, smaller group that strains to supply the revenue for basic governmental services. Faced with the declining number of young families and a plant that no longer takes its students, the schools are plagued by low enrollment, a small revenue base, and the full cost of a single district's overhead. The Steelton design, of a model nineteenth-century industrial town, is no longer needed and is clearly headed for extinction.

While there are a variety of band-aid solutions that could help Steelton limp along for a few more years, the real need is to *transform Steelton into a town that serves the needs of the coming century* and *gives it a direction* that will allow real growth and unsubsidized prosperity. What we need to do is put ourselves in the mindset of those men of 1865 Philadelphia and create the *NEW BALDWIN.*

This statement also presented a challenge to the community. A concept brief stated the need to form a coalition of government, labor, business, community, and education leaders into the "New Baldwin Project." The project would attempt to convert Steelton into a prototype twenty-first century industrial/manufacturing community. The defined project mission was to integrate key community segments (e.g., government, labor) into a new organizational model that would maximize the ability of the community to compete globally and to provide advanced standards of living for residents.

One section of the report identified basic problems that seriously threatened the future of Steelton and its citizens. These included lack of vision, shared goals, and strategic planning, outmoded, fragmented and uncoordinated government agencies, inadequately educated students, business organizations that block innovation and quick response to customers, and lack of reinvestment to modernize production processes and equipment. The report predicted that unless these problems were dealt with effectively, Steelton would become "a ghost town without decent employment, no local education system, and a poverty-ridden populace begging for government support."

The report also presented a preliminary vision that held out hope for the future. Elements of the vision included:

- An advisory board or steering committee that would represent all stakeholders with working committees for specific issues.
- The development of Bethlehem Steel property as a "base site" for an Enterprise Zone.
- School districts and higher education to spearhead a twenty-first-century educational program to develop the technical/knowledge worker.
- Organized labor to explore new ways of organization and promote leading edge work organizations.
- Government organizations to reexamine roles, structures, and authority to streamline and focus government services.
- An educational, research, technology and human resources focus dedicated to leading edge industrial/manufacturing ideas.
- Funding and maximum integration of various organizations, groups, and institutions.

Convening Community Members

Ike Gittlen used his membership in the Capital Area Labor Management Council to present his proposal to the general community. In February 1992, the council called a meeting that provided a forum for presenting and discussing the proposal. The approximately 60 business, labor, political, education, community, and economic development leaders attending the meeting supported the formation of the New Baldwin Project and accepted the concepts included in Ike's report as the basis for developing a twenty-first-century manufacturing community. They also supported the formation of a steering committee (Pasmore, 1988) to guide network activities and development (see Figure 2.1) and to form committees to stimulate thinking and initiate work in several key areas, among them education, workplace competitiveness, sociotechnical research, intergovernmental cooperation. These committees of six to eight members began meeting regularly and provided many ideas and considerable energy to the network during the first two years of work. By providing a way of allowing many interested persons to become directly involved in coalition work through small group discussions, the committees made an important contribution to establishing and developing the network. Figure 2.2 illustrates the work of the socio-technical research committee.

A steering committee (SC) includes representatives of stakeholder organizations and groups involved in the network. In principle, all groups and organizations that (1) can contribute to devising a solution or (2) will be affected by working on a large-scale problem should be included. Ideally, SC members have enough authority to speak for their organizations and commit them to network decisions.

A steering committee does the following:

1. Governs the network.

2. Guides network activities and network development.

3. Links the network continuously to member organizations and the larger outside environment.

Figure 2.1
Network Steering Committee

Mission

The socio-technical research committee provides research and generates ideas which support the overall mission and direction of the New Baldwin Corridor Coalition. It acts both as a "think tank" and as a resource responding the requests generated by other coalition committees. Its research thrust covers five primary areas:

1. Social and technical systems development; structure, culture and operation of organizations that can bring about the coalition's vision;

2. Technological change, how applications of technologies combined with human systems design can create competitive industries and increase the quality of life in the Corridor;

3. Markets for products and services that can be offered by industries operating in the Corridor and those that fit the strategic plant to be developed by the coalition;

4. Models of other networks in communities that have begun or completed a transformation similar to that envisioned by the coalition; and

Figure 2.2
Mission Statement and Activities of the Socio-Technical Research Committee (continued)

Figure 2.2 *(continued)*

5. Action research on the progress of developing the NBCC and components of the coalition to provide short-term feedback for assessing progress, changing plans based on new information, and learning from experience.

Activities

The committee carries out its mission by engaging in the following types of activities:

1. Keeping the coalition informed about what has happened in similar projects in other countries. What can we learn from these projects that will help make expectations realistic and help make planning/implementation effective?

2. Conducting research on existing organizations and on industry opportunities that may have application in the corridor. Particular attention will be given to identifying industry clusters which have the potential to create and maintain meaningful employment in the corridor.

3. Chronicling and helping to evaluate the organizing, implementing, and managing of coalition development.

4. Providing information and direction to the coalition on new forms of organization, management, and training required to compete in the international marketplace and provide high-quality employment to the area workforce.

5. Conducting research on technologies and their applications by targeted and existing industries. Emphasis will be placed on identifying potential centers of excellence, synthesizing information from existing centers of research and technology, and expanding that body of research to shape the vision of the New Baldwin Project.

6. Developing basic designs on principles and application of sociotechnical systems, network development, labor-management collaboration, and other topics crucial to building the coalition.

7. Providing an inventory of research needs of the coalition. Research needs include technical, human, and organizational requirements.

8. Involving engineers, technicians, and technology managers from area organizations in discussing and developing recommendations on technological issues.

Reactions after the meeting were encouraging. A Harrisburg *Patriot-News* article called the proposal "futuristic" and "visionary" and a local politician indicated that "It's a call to leaders to act like leaders." While other reactions were more cautious, the proposal had struck a responsive chord in the community.

During the next two months, work centered on broadening membership in the coalition. Coalition work took place in steering committee and general monthly meetings, committees, and ad hoc small group meetings of network members. Open general monthly meetings usually attracted 40 to 50 persons from diverse groups and organizations. These included business organizations, labor unions, local, state, and federal government, community organizations and residents, education, and economic development organizations. Meetings involved high levels of interaction among steering committee members, special guests, community residents, and representatives of various organizations. Participants in the discussion experienced a sense of excitement, a feeling that "We're part of something important that's creating a new community!" The specific format and content of meetings varied with the key issues facing the coalition and decisions that required action.

By the end of April 1992, the project had started to function as a new network organization. It held meetings, made decisions, took action, and attained some recognition in the larger community. At the April general meeting, participants decided to expand its boundary beyond Steelton to include the 13-mile corridor from the Harrisburg International Airport 10 miles south of the city to the north side of town. Until this time, thinking had focused primarily on the borough of Steelton, due to the great impact of the Bethlehem plant on the local community. General meetings convened originally as the Steelton Community Coalition showed this thinking. Boundary expansion resulted from recognizing existing interdependencies among area organizations and the scope of development work required to bring about change. It also helped give the network the critical mass required for its work. For example, the new boundary included the city of Harrisburg and seven other municipalities. Extending the boundary also incorporated Penn State Harrisburg and Harrisburg Area Community College, two strong supporters of the coalition, within the network. Adopting a new name, the New Baldwin Corridor Coalition, reflected the expanded boundary.

During the first three months of existence, the new network organization also adopted a mission statement. According to this original statement, the coalition identified the following goals:

1. Establish a coalition of government, labor, community, business, and education leaders.
2. Involve every regional institution in the creation of a proto-typical twenty-first-century community that can compete globally and provide an advanced standard of living.
3. Acknowledge the need for major cultural change in our institutions and ourselves. Accept the need to think differently about how we deal with and solve problems.
4. Prove that existing communities can convert to meet global realities.
5. Focus on business revival, educational integration, human resource issues, governmental restructuring, housing and human services, and research and technology.

In essence, the statement defined a need for systemic change to occur through the involvement of all basic organizations and institutions in the community. It also indicated that a new form of organization and new ways of thinking and operating would be required.

Developing the Coalition

Conceptualizing Network Development

When I began working with New Baldwin in 1992, my first two months' activity involved becoming familiar with coalition work and developing links with other members. Much of the learning and relationship building occurred via my participating in meetings as a steering committee member and chairing the socio-technical research committee. At first, the fast pace of a variety of activities by many different groups and individuals made it difficult to get a feel for New Baldwin and how I could contribute to its development. But it was impossible to avoid being caught up in the pervasive air of excitement. So I hung on and trusted that sufficient understanding and clarity would emerge.

As I became familiar with the network, four questions surfaced:

1. What is the nature of the NBCC? Both members and non-members were confused about its exact nature. A natural inclination was to think of the coalition as a traditional organization based on mechanistic principles of bureaucracy (i.e., hierarchy, fixed jurisdictions). But these principles were inconsistent with the spirit and vision of New Baldwin.

2. What is the role of the coalition? A member raised this issue early in a general meeting by asking "What can we do that existing organizations can't?" This statement captured two conflicting feelings: (a) that New Baldwin would just be like other organizations and would not make a difference in changing the community; and (b) that New Baldwin would succeed and threaten the existence of some member organizations.

3. Will business organizations support the network? A number of business organizations had supported NBCC from the beginning. However, coalition members perceived that a lack of involvement by a sufficient number of businesses posed a threat to the network.

4. How will the coalition be funded? What sources of funds will provide revenues to develop and maintain New Baldwin as an interorganizational network and enable it to carry out its work? Although the organization has made progress in addressing these issues since early 1992, they continue in varying degrees to the present time.

Reflecting on the first question caused me to think about concepts, approaches, and principles that would contribute to understanding the nature of the coalition and processes to support its development. Two key ideas stemmed from this reflection. The first was Trist's conceptualization of socio-ecological networks described in Chapter 1, which seemed a close fit for the nature, vision, and mission of New Baldwin. Bringing together a diverse set of organizations to address a critical issue by creating a higher level vision and developing shared ways of bringing the vision into being seemed to be the essence of New Baldwin. Second, it became clear that using an action research (AR) process (See Figure 2.3) would be required to develop the coalition as a network organization. I concluded that continuous cycles of diagnosing, planning, implementing action steps, collecting data on outcomes and the state of the system, and planning new cycles of action would be required to develop the system (Chisholm, 1997; Lewin, 1946; Susman and Evered, 1978). It also seemed clear that short cycles of taking action, sharing experiences, and drawing conclusions would be necessary for organizational learning to occur. I also established links with innovative network development work being done by colleagues in Norway, Sweden, and other parts of the United States, and began discussing the project with them whenever possible.

Action research (AR) is an approach to organization development, not a specific technique. Essentially, it attempts to generate knowledge about a network as an integral part of the development process. AR involves repeated cycles of diagnosis, planning, implementing, collecting and analyzing outcome data, reviewing and discussing data and reflections with network members, reaching conclusions, and defining new sets of action plans. The diagram shown here depicts the AR process.

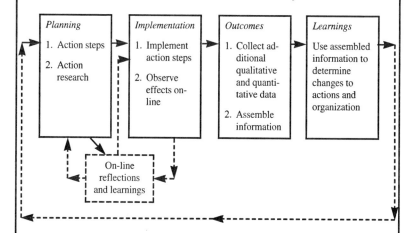

Using an action research approach for network development extends well beyond using planned, clearly identifiable information feedback processes. Over time, devising ways of determining the effects of plans, activities, and actions should become part of how the network organization functions. Network members should devise ways of determining outcomes automatically as a natural part of conducting work and managing the network development process. An AR perspective means that individuals are constantly asking questions:

1. What needs to be done to make the shared vision a reality and reach the defined goals?.

2. How can we identify the *real effects* of plans and actions?

3. What changes must be made based upon feedback about actual outcomes?

Figure 2.3
Action Research for Network Development (continued)

Figure 2.3 *(continued)*

4. What have we learned from previous cycles of goal setting, planning, implementation?

5. How are learnings from earlier work made part of how the developing network operates?

Establishing the value of AR is basic to developing a network organization. The AR process reinforces the concept of the organization as a learning system. It also underlines the transiency of specific goals, plans, activities, and organization arrangements and highlights differences between espoused and actual values and guiding principles. Through the AR approach, members obtain information about actual outcomes of earlier decisions that enable them to learn from these for the future and make necessary adjustments.

Expanding Understanding of Guiding Concepts

After identifying the socio-ecological network perspective and action research as crucial to developing the system, I looked for ways to use these two constructs to advance coalition development. The socio-ecological view of networks provided the concepts needed to help network members answer the first two questions posed in the previous section regarding the nature of NBCC and its role. And, the action research process offered a possible way of involving various groups in coalition work and its outcomes. In short, action research offered a potential means for addressing the other two issues identified above: (1) expanding involvement of business organizations and (2) generating funding to support the coalition.

Steering committee concern about the lack of active involvement of enough business leaders in coalition work was noted above. Consequently, the steering committee asked a highly respected coalition member with extensive business contacts to interview a small number of top managers and executives in the region during early summer of 1992. Thirty individuals from 20 organizations and three nonprofit associations participated in the survey. Open-ended interview questions covered strengths and limitations of the area, perceptions of New Baldwin, and related topics important for economic and social development. Responses were analyzed and presented in August at an expanded steering committee meeting that approximately forty-five persons attended. Responses were also used in several later presentations to business, labor, and community groups and in starting to plan New Baldwin activities. Hence the survey represented an early, naturally occurring rough use of action research to help guide coalition work.

Results of the survey (see Table 2.1) indicated that managers perceived several basic advantages of the New Baldwin corridor. These included the convergence of several interstate highways at

---

NBCC Advantages
- Highway system
- Public transportation
- Airport
- Higher education availability
- Utilities available—water, sewer, steam
- Skilled labor
- Freight transportation
- Industrial land available

NBCC Disadvantages
- Much of land is located in a floodplain
- Environmental problems and undefined financial liability from using old industrial sites
- Small, cut-up parcels of land
- Vandalism and security
- Some employees unreliable—absenteeism, tardiness, turnover
- Access roads
- Local government officials unresponsive

Opportunities
- Assist existing business
- Access roads
- Search for land development
- Develop light rail system (long range)

Observations of NBCC
- Lack of business input and leadership; perceived union dominance a negative
- Too many meetings
- Not focused, too many projects
- Duplicating existing organizations
- Need a short-term "success"

Table 2.1
Outcomes of a Survey of Business Leaders

Harrisburg, abundant freight transportation via truck and rail, air service at an international airport, skilled labor, higher education, and available industrial land. Disadvantages included the location of some industrial sites in a floodplain and the environmental hazards that plague "old" manufacturing sites, the unresponsiveness of local government officials, and the lack of access roads. Managers also raised questions about the coalition. For example, conservative managers asked how involved they should become in an effort initiated by a union leader. They also expressed concerns about setting up a group that might duplicate the work of existing organizations, and, they were wary of having too many meetings and an unfocused agenda.

In late spring, the director of the Penn State Downtown Center asked me to give a presentation on NBCC in September. I agreed, provided it would be an Ike and Rupe presentation; Ike readily consented. As the originator and visionary of the coalition, Ike could talk authoritatively about its history and vision. I also knew the excitement he generated in individuals who heard him speak about the coalition. My role would be to help participants understand New Baldwin as an interorganizational network and to help them learn about the action research approach to developing the system. Feeding back a summary of findings from the business manager survey was a natural way of illustrating one application of action research. Another aim of this approach was to demonstrate the coalition as a learning organization, as illustrated in Figure 2.4 (Argyris and Schön, 1996; Senge, 1990).

A group of approximately 50 individuals, including managers and professionals from state government agencies, attended our presentation. Ike Gittlen recounted the history, vision, mission, and early development of New Baldwin. I described the basic action research process and used findings from the business survey to illustrate one way of using the approach to develop the coalition. I also described several key features of the NBCC as a network organization.

Participants expressed interest in the coalition and asked many questions about it and its development. Since the session was videotaped and was replayed many times on a local educational TV channel, it also helped inform residents of the general community about the coalition as an interorganizational network and about the action research approach being used. Anecdotal evidence indicated that a number of community members became interested in New Baldwin through this medium.

General feedback on the downtown presentation was positive. After the meeting, one participant asked me about repeating the presen-

Building the capacity of the three networks described in Chapters 2–8 as learning organizations was a meta-goal of development work. Argyris and Schön (1996, pp. xviii–xix) have captured the essence of networks as learning systems:

> In all areas of social action, there has evolved a powerful image of organizations caught up in reciprocal transactions with the environments in which they are embedded. Organizational success, however defined, is seen as depending on the organization's ability to see things in new ways—all on a continuing basis and in a way that engages the organization as a whole.

In short, in learning organizations, learning becomes a way of life at all levels—individual, group, department, organization. And a legitimate concern of all action or contemplated action is "what can we learn from this," not just "what have we accomplished." This focus on learning is essential to increase network capacity (and that of members) to respond to future events and to generate new knowledge that is useful in an ever-changing world.

Increasing network capacity for learning requires several things:

1. *Valuing:* Establishing and maintaining the value of learning as a legitimate continuous activity.

2. *Norming:* Fostering the emergence of behavior patterns and expectations that support continuous learning.

3. *Developing:* Integrating learning as part of action research into all network development interventions. This helps demonstrate the value of learning and foster emergence of norms that support it.

Ideally, over time, learning becomes a key part of the network culture.

Figure 2.4
Networks as Learning Organizations

tation to coalition members at the next general meeting. Her suggestion was accepted by the chair of the steering committee and a second presentation on network and action research concepts took place at the general NBCC meeting in October. Observations and feedback indicated that this presentation helped increase understanding of the nature of New Baldwin as a network organization and of the action research process supporting its development. Still, much work remained to be done.

Strategic Planning Conference

During the summer of 1992, steering committee members became increasingly aware of the need to broaden involvement in the coalition. Feedback from the business leaders survey clearly indicated this need, and contacts with other parts of the community revealed a continuing lack of information and understanding of New Baldwin. Consequently, the steering committee decided in early November to convene a community search process to respond to these needs. Details of this conference appear in the next chapter.

Conclusion: The State of the Coalition in August 1992

Six months of working with NBCC led me to several conclusions:

- Ike's vision was powerful and had tapped a sensitive nerve in the community. People were moved by it.
- Many individuals from various sectors shared Ike's view about the plight of the community and appeared to agree that a new collaborative approach was needed to change the situation.
- Leaders from government, labor, business, education, community, and health care organizations had demonstrated support for the coalition by participating in early meetings.
- Local residents had shown support by attending general meetings and special sessions.

Despite these positive signs, several previously identified issues remained to be dealt with. These included:

- *The nature of New Baldwin:* As indicated earlier, coalition members and those in the community were unclear about what NBCC was and tended to think of it as a traditional organization.
- *The role of the coalition:* Individuals were unclear about what New Baldwin could add to what was already being done.
- *Business involvement:* Despite participation in the business survey, continuous active involvement of firms in NBCC work remained unclear.

- *Funding:* How would New Baldwin obtain sufficient funds to coordinate activities, maintain communication among members and with the community, and conduct network development work?

These observations summarize the state of New Baldwin in late summer 1992. They also provide the context for the major network development intervention covered in Chapter 3.

3

The Strategic Planning Conference: A Major Step in Developing the Coalition

Introducing the Idea

The possibility of using a search conference or search process to advance Coalition development emerged during the summer of 1992. From participation in a workshop several years earlier, discussions with colleagues, and reading, the search conference stood out as a potential process for broadening stakeholder involvement, increasing understanding of New Baldwin, and identifying broad areas of work. First, I began discussing the idea of conducting a community search conference informally with Ike. His reaction was lukewarm at best. He showed a bit of interest but had serious reservations about the willingness of stakeholder representatives to participate, our ability to design and conduct it successfully, and outcomes. (Frankly, I wasn't completely sure it would work either but thought it deserved a careful look).

Serendipity led to the second step in introducing and gaining support for the search conference idea. My colleague and friend, Thoralf Qvale, of the Work Research Institute in Oslo was planning to attend the Academy of Management meeting in August. So, I suggested to Ike that we try to use this visit as a way of getting an experienced outsider's view of NBCC and its development. Thoralf had some general understanding of New Baldwin from brief phone conversations with me. His potential visit seemed likely to provide several positives:

1. A professional cross-check on my reading of the situation and possible next steps;
2. A chance for the coalition to get a fresh perspective and new ideas from an experienced outsider; and

3. A new forum for Ike and Rupe to discuss New Baldwin and the development process.

Thoralf had spent a sabbatical at Penn State in State College, Pennsylvania, in 1989–1990, during which he had met Ike. Ike respected him, thought having him spend time with us was a good idea, and quickly agreed to it.

A fax to Thoralf in Oslo revealed that he was on a sailing vacation in the North Sea. Fortunately, he got the message and phoned back a few days later. After discussing what we had in mind, he expressed eagerness to meet with us and indicated that he would attempt to rearrange his schedule. On the Saturday morning following the Academy conference, Ike, Thoralf, and I met at I.W. Abel Hall, the Steelworkers' Union building. During the meeting, we reviewed the status of New Baldwin, ideas about its development, and similar

---

A search conference uses the open systems principle that understanding an organization requires starting with the environment and working inward. This approach helps to open participants' thinking, ensure that useful general information about the environment is considered, and build bridges across existing organizational boundaries. Search conferences are designed primarily to catalyze change by having stakeholders engage in an open process of exploring what the future might be and stimulating participants to create it. Properly designed and managed, a search conference provides a unique forum in which a diverse set of participants meets to deal with broad network issues in nontraditional ways.

Consistent with OD principles, a search conference rests on the assumption that the individuals, organizations, and groups that have a direct stake in a broad problem or issue must provide the energy for change by becoming deeply involved in the development process. The search process also assumes that they have the in-depth knowledge required for successful change. Although specialized expert knowledge and information usually is required during the change process, this expertise should respond to general guidance and requests from the stakeholders rather than drive the development process. In short, search conferences are designed to "help people restructure their views of reality to see beyond the superficial conditions and events into the underlying causes of problems—and therefore to see new possibilities for shaping the future" (Senge, 1990, p. 24).

Figure 3.1
Search Conference (continued)

Figure 3.1 *(continued)*

A typical search conference involves five phases of activity that comprise part of a holistic process. The fifth phase of the process carries over to designing and managing activities selected for attention during the conference itself. As the following diagram of a search conference on economic/social community development indicates, foci of the phases funnel down from a highly general exploration of the environment (phase 1) to general action steps to bring about the "desired future" (phase 5).

Phases in the Search Conference Process

Preconference Activities
Designing and Planning Conference

PHASE 1 *Exploring the General Environment*
Focal Issue: Trends or forces that will affect the U.S. economy during the next 10 years

PHASE 2 *Identifying Current Community Situation*
Focal Issue: Key features—both positive and negative—of this community and its history.

PHASE 3 *Visioning a Desirable Future*
Focal Issue: Creating a shared vision of an ideal community future.

PHASE 4 *Planning Broad Action Steps*
Focal Issue: Creating a strategy and defining goals and strategy to progress toward ideal future. Establish task forces on key issues identified.

PHASE 5 *Following Through: Post-Conference Work*
Focal Issue: Conducting project work to implement plans and strategy.
Maintaining the network organization as an effective system.

PHASE 1 engages members of the total group in a broad exploration of the environment. Emphasis is placed on the future, and discussion of the past is excluded. A broad open-ended question, such as "What trends will affect the U.S. economy during the next 10 years?" elicits participants' perceptions of trends in technical, values, attitudes, political, economic, demographic and other critical areas. Following creative thinking guidelines for exploring issues, critical judgment is suspended and all alternatives identified are simply listed without being evaluated.

Figure 3.1 *(continued)*

Using these guidelines is crucial to demonstrate the importance of everyone's inputs and to help ensure that all key environmental trends are included.

PHASE 2 turns attention to perceived positive and negative aspects of the community as it now exists. Responding to a question such as "What are key features—both positive and negative—of this community and what is its history?" builds a shared picture of the system as it actually exists. Focusing discussion on positive and negative features of the system also helps root the search process in reality and helps ensure that valued unique features become incorporated in the emerging vision of a "desirable future."

PHASE 3 focuses on "What could be" in the community. This discussion builds on future trends identified during the exploration of the general environment (phase 1) and the reality testing of the existing system that occurred during the second phase. Developing several visions also elicits a set of values: These emerge implicitly as group members discuss possible alternative futures. Selection of general features of a shared vision of the future occurs in response to addressing "What character do we want the community/region to have?" The shared vision serves as a superordinate purpose that helps develop collaboration among potentially competing organizations.

PHASE 4 identifies basic steps to take to begin creating a community or region with the desired characteristics. Discussion centers on future trends, constraints and opportunities of the actual initiatives, and the values expressed during earlier stages of the search process. It is crucial to discuss these areas adequately so that agreed upon steps to create the desired future balance of ideal, realistic, and value considerations.

PHASE 5 represents an extension of the discussion process from the previous phase. Now, attention focuses on what action to take to implement the general vision agreed upon in phase 4. Typically, task forces or project teams are formed to follow up on general action steps identified during the previous phase. Follow-up activities generated here usually continue long after the search conference has ended.

Traditional search conferences require two or three days. However, alternate designs for "searching" are possible and the exact amount of time required depends on design decisions, time constraints, and how events unfold during the actual search process.

efforts in other places. Thoralf asked many questions and shared some of his experiences in assisting with network development. Toward the end of the meeting, he mentioned that convening a search conference (see Figure 3.1) might be a useful developmental step in the next six months or so. We discussed the idea a bit, but not in great detail. General conversation over lunch ended the meeting.

The idea of holding a search conference (Emery and Emery, 1978; Emery and Purser, 1996; Weisbord, 1992) lay dormant for several weeks. Ike and I discussed our meeting with Thoralf briefly, and we probably talked about the idea of a search conference. But nothing more was done immediately. Then, in mid-September, Ike began to talk informally with me about it. The conversation was exploratory and tentative, but Ike was showing more interest in the idea. He also mentioned it once or twice in passing during conversations with several steering committee members. Overall, relatively little discussion about a search conference occurred during the next few weeks.

Sponsoring a Search Conference

The steering committee made a decision to sponsor some type of conference at our November 2, 1992 meeting. The stated purpose of the meeting was to review the status of the business survey and plan ways of conducting additional surveys among other key coalition groups. The excerpts shown in Figure 3.2 capture the flow of the meeting and its changing focus.

Continuing Existing Approach

Ike suggested that all current surveys in progress should carry on. We should work to gather baseline information by integration and coordination of the survey. A plan and strategy up front will minimize time and work and increase the quality of outcomes.

Three key questions need to be answered by area businesses:

1. What is your goal?
2. How do you expect to achieve your goal?
3. What help or support do you need? (technology, education, government, etc.)

Figure 3.2
The Winding Road to a Decision (continued)
Source: New Baldwin Corridor Steering Committee Notes, Business Survey Meeting, November 2, 1992. Headings provided by author.

Figure 3.2 *(continued)*

Questioning Current Approach

Pat said we may need to do separate surveys, but they need to be integrated and not be the same old questions that do not view the whole picture. Pat also suggested that the schools' strategic planning may not deal with or answer what we need...

An outside survey research expert invited to the meeting asked:

1. What information is it really necessary for you to know?
2. How are data to be used?

Suggesting a New Approach

Pat suggested doing a roundtable discussion with a mission statement, an agenda, and specific goals to be provided in an overview at the beginning of the session. Use a facilitator and invite good participants (10–12).

Rupe suggested that a search conference could be up to 80 participants (or more).

Fran said each committee has different needs, input is necessary from all areas.

Pat suggested hand picking several people from each committee area.

Tammy stressed that community members need to be included as well.

Rupe suggested mixing a representative from each area in one group.

Solidifying New Approach

Ike said that if we plan for an organized meeting and discussion with a well-organized agenda, outcomes will happen and this will serve as our survey.

Nature of the Conference

Pat said after the overview break up into separate groups for several hours. Then regroup and report out. Take info back into three larger groups to prioritize and define.

Types needed to attend: Borough managers, shop floor supervisors, bankers, lawyers, teachers, and a few CEO, business owner, union president types.

Figure 3.2 *(continued)*

Carry this out in January—middle of the month and use info to report on at an Annual Meeting in February.

Need expression from each committee to use in the overview and agenda and a list of names, eight or so from each group (need some extras, to be used if someone cannot attend).

Target groups with names should be complete by 11/24/92. Invitations will be sent out to specific individuals and back up phone calls will be made to ascertain attendance. Committee will decide replacement names for those unable to attend.

Six participants will meet again next week.

While the SC decision to use a search process was exciting ("They have listened and understood!"), several aspects of it caused serious concern:

- *Timing:* Mid-January! That's impossible! How can we possibly pull this off so quickly?

- *Understanding:* Do SC members have sufficient understanding of what a search process can do? Can it really meet their expectations?

- *Commitment:* Were members really committed to this or was the decision rushed prematurely? Had I been sucked into this also?

- *Design:* They're getting too involved with details of the design.

- *Resources:* Do we have the professional competence, financial, and other resources to make this successful?

- *Confrontation:* Okay, big mouth! You got your wish, now you've got to deliver! or "Be careful of your wish; it may be granted!"

In any event, a decision had been made and there was nothing to do but to make something positive from the opportunity.

Design Process

The process of designing and planning the conference took place over a ten-week period. This was an extremely short time span considering the size and nature of the event. As a result, many different individuals and groups participated in various aspects of the work.

Figure 3.3 gives key steps in the process of designing the NBCC strategic planning meeting. Ten days after the SC decision to hold a conference, several committee members met to clarify think-

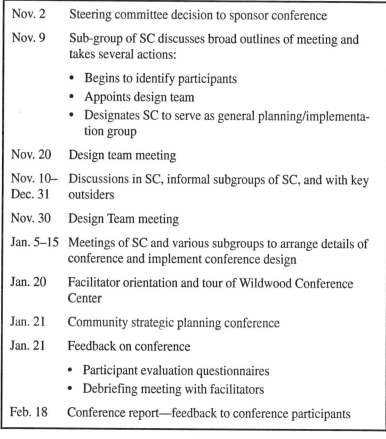

Nov. 2	Steering committee decision to sponsor conference
Nov. 9	Sub-group of SC discusses broad outlines of meeting and takes several actions:
	• Begins to identify participants
	• Appoints design team
	• Designates SC to serve as general planning/implementation group
Nov. 20	Design team meeting
Nov. 10– Dec. 31	Discussions in SC, informal subgroups of SC, and with key outsiders
Nov. 30	Design Team meeting
Jan. 5–15	Meetings of SC and various subgroups to arrange details of conference and implement conference design
Jan. 20	Facilitator orientation and tour of Wildwood Conference Center
Jan. 21	Community strategic planning conference
Jan. 21	Feedback on conference
	• Participant evaluation questionnaires
	• Debriefing meeting with facilitators
Feb. 18	Conference report—feedback to conference participants

Figure 3.3
Key Steps in Design Process for NBCC Strategic Planning Conference

---

Network development work covered in this book made extensive use of design teams. These were small groups (3–7 members) that met to design and plan a specific intervention in the network development process. The team usually included me, and often another OD professional, and several network members. Using design teams was intended to achieve several goals:

1. Improve the quality of designs by combining network members' in-depth knowledge of the networks, their organizations, and the external environment with OD professionals' understanding of change and system development.

2. Ensure that network members retained control of the development process; that they, not OD specialists, were responsible for and taking charge of change.

3. Advance learning of all team members from wrestling with design issues, making decisions, and planning interventions.

4. Have learning through doing become a way of life in the network.

Figure 3.4
Design Team

ing and devise a plan for designing and making the event happen. Several decisions resulted from this meeting:

- *Identifying participants:* Requested each committee to prepare a list of recommended participants.
- *Form design team:* Selected a small group of representatives from various coalition member organizations to develop a general design for the conference; I was asked to chair this team.
- *Planning implementation:* Decided that the steering committee would serve as the general planning and implementation group.

First Design Team Meeting

Six members attended the first Design Team (See Figure 3.4) meeting on November 20. I designed and chaired the meeting. To help ground discussion, the meeting began with a short review of "Where do we stand in developing the NBCC?" Dealing with this question was intended to do several things:

- Emphasize the ongoing need to devote attention and resources to developing and maintaining the coalition.
- Get design team members to assess where the coalition stood in its development and where the strategic planning meeting would fit in the overall process.
- Gain understanding that individuals attending the conference who had not previously been involved with New Baldwin would have much less knowledge and understanding than "veterans." Conference design must also consider this.

Discussion then turned to defining the purpose of the meeting. After generating many ideas, the team stated a three-part purpose:

1. Creating a forum for an open exchange of views about the coalition;
2. Advancing development and understanding of New Baldwin as a network organization; and
3. Determining needs of coalition stakeholders within the context of the network vision of the total community.

Design team members also identified a list of issues that had to be addressed in designing the conference. As Figure 3.5 shows, the team gave recommendations, information, or opinions on several topics. Members also defined a key general design issue: How would we mesh the information generating need with the need to develop the coalition and ensure that all participants have a chance to influence its future development?

Toward the end of the meeting, I used a few descriptive comments to acquaint team members with the nature of the search process. These included stating characteristics of the search process:

- *It is future oriented.* What do we (the participants) want to make happen?
- *It is holistic.* Orients thinking to the total system.
- *It is vision based.* Relates activity to a shared vision that puts values front and center.
- *It includes representatives from all key organizations involved.*
- *It creates conditions for open dialogue.*
- *It validates everyone's reality.* Acknowledges differences but does not address them.

- Organizations to invite? What organizations are critical to NBCC success?
  Education—public, higher
  Government—federal, state, local
  Business—large, small
  Labor—locals, regional, state
  Community residents—include churches
  Health care(?)
  Financial community—banks, real estate, etc.
  Agriculture (from ecological and land use perspective)

- Representative of each organization; decision makers in formal organizations; opinion leaders in community.

- Who convenes the event and issues official invitations? Should be high-profile person accepted and respected by all constituents.

- What is done (content)?

- IIow? Establish a process for real discussion and dialogue to occur

- Amount of time: 1/2 day, 1 day, 1 1/2 days, etc.?

- How to communicate event to participants; personal invitations will be needed

- How to cover conference costs—e.g., coffee, lunch, mailing, materials, etc.

- Location—where to hold meeting?

- Facilities—rooms, equipment, etc.?

- Timing—mid-January—This date seems overly optimistic.

- Day of week

- Time of day

Figure 3.5
Key Design Issues for NBCC Strategic Planning Conference

I also outlined the basic phases of the search process and a brief discussion followed. Team members responded positively to this approach to designing and conducting the conference.

Informal Discussions and Second Design Team Meeting

Informal discussions among various individuals and groups between meetings played a crucial role in developing the design and plans for the conference. For example, Ike talked with two leaders of the business community about the general design. These individuals were convinced that business leaders would be unwilling to participate in a meeting that lasted longer than a half day—perhaps we could stretch it to 5 1/2 hours by scheduling it from 7:30 a.m. to 1:00 p.m., including lunch. Ike and I discussed this and concluded that, although it was far from ideal, we could do something productive in the time period. According to our rough calculations, a useful allocation of time might be 1/2 hour for orientation, 3 hours for small group discussions, 1/2 hour for breaks, 1/2 hour lost time for moves, and 1 hour for a working lunch.

Meanwhile, Pat, another SC member, had checked on availability of the Wildwood Conference Center at Harrisburg Area Community College. The center met basic criteria for the conference site: neutral location; comfortable and attractive facilities; capacity to handle a large group meeting and multiple concurrent small group sessions; convenient location with ample parking. Other coalition members were working on many other aspects of the conference (e.g., identifying conference participants; fund-raising). Steering committee review of design team recommendations and information from various sources inside and outside the coalition provided further input to the design process.

The design team met a second time on November 30. As indicated above, several things had occurred since the first meeting to begin to crystallize overall conference design. These factors plus the pressure of time spurred the team to develop a specific proposed outline for the conference. Details of the proposal included a date (Thursday, January 21, 1993); location (Wildwood Conference Center); and theme ("Inventing Ways to Make the NBCC Globally Competitive").

The features of the proposed design were as follows:

- *Opening of the meeting:* Brief remarks by notables, vision and short history of NBCC, overview of day and guidelines.

- *Three periods of concurrent small group meetings:*
  Heterogeneous, with representatives from all stakeholders
  Discussion takes place on an assigned broad question(s) for each meeting period
  A trained facilitator to work with each group to ease and focus discussion and record comments on flip charts
- *General session and lunch*
  Sharing of selected highlights from small group sessions
  Identify requirements for Coalition to take next steps
- *Sequence of questions:* The form of questions would flow from the most general (e.g., environmental trends/pressures) to the most specific (e.g., what actions should be taken) per search process design principles.

The design team also identified and discussed several other issues.

- *Key facilitator:* The subcommittee recommended using an outside facilitator to manage the meeting. This person would work closely with me to monitor overall developments and make desired changes that responded to developments during the meeting.
- *Collecting data and reproduction:* Use laptop computers to record information gathered by facilitators during small group sessions if possible.
- *Arrangements*
- *Invitations:* Leaders of various sectors; identify who will issue and how:
  Committee recommends phone call or personal visit, followed up by a letter.
  Decide on stationery and enclosures
- *Small group facilitators*
  Five to six potential small group facilitators were identified (several more were needed)
  Need to orient before meeting
- *Coordination:* Who coordinates meeting?
  Rupe for design aspects (e.g., size of rooms, seating arrangements)
  Identify other persons to handle many administrative details including hospitality arrangements, publicity, and handouts at meeting

Planning and Implementing the Design

By mid-December the basic design for the meeting was set and much work had taken place to plan the conference. At this point, attention began to center on following through on existing plans, generating additional detailed action steps, and ensuring that all key activities were taking place. Hence, the steering committee held a series of meetings to work out detailed plans, assign responsibility to various groups and individuals, monitor progress, and make required adjustments.

Basic conference design decisions included three detailed planning areas crucial to success:

1. *Small group discussions:* This decision required locating a conference facility that would have enough breakout rooms to handle 8 to 10 small groups and that would also meet other basic conference requirements. A small-group format also required planning/follow-through to ensure that physical, social, and technical needs (e.g., room arrangement, equipment, noise level) would be met. If heterogeneous groups were formed, it would be necessary to assign individuals to groups and adjust assignments at the conference based on who actually attended.

2. *Facilitators:* The decision to use facilitators required identifying qualified individuals, obtaining their agreement to participate in the conference pro bono, and orienting them to the conference and their role in it.

3. *Time period:* Limiting the conference to 5 1/2 hours led to several other decisions to help prepare participants before they arrived and conserve time during the conference. These included mailing participants background information on NBCC and a list of conference discussion issues and questions several days before the conference. Using trained facilitators, developing guidelines and ground rules to help guide and focus discussions, and managing time carefully by having a general facilitator to help keep things moving also contributed to effective use of time. Again, each basic design decision had ripple effects on later decisions and planning/implementation work.

Carrying out the detailed planning/implementation work resulted in developing checklists of work and identifying individuals responsible for conducting it. The steering committee identified required work, obtained agreement from various individuals to carry

Task	Person Responsible
Workshop lists and mailings	Tammy (Administrative Assistant)
Follow-up letter	Ike
Facilitators—recruit, orient	Rupe
Conference folders for participants	Tammy
Speakers	Frank, Chair, NBCC
Program agenda, guidelines/ ground rules	Rupe
Registration and small group assignments	Carol and 2 volunteers
Packet assembly	Tammy, Carol, Bob K.
Press conference-preparation	Larry, Paul
Press conference-participants	Fran, Ike, SC members

Figure 3.6
Selected Items from Strategic Planning Meeting Checklist

out the work, monitored progress, and coordinated the work. An administrative assistant from the Capital Area Labor Management Council provided strong support and coordinated much of the planning. Selected items from one checklist (see Figure 3.6) illustrate the variety of detailed planning activities and number of individuals and groups involved. Volunteers came from many different organizations, which showed strong general support from the community.

The Conference

As planned, the Strategic Planning Conference was held on January 21, 1993. A total of 96 individuals participated in the conference with fairly equal numbers of representatives from key constituent groups (27 business, 19 government, 19 education, 16 labor, and 15 community representatives).

Figure 3.7 illustrates the final program of the meeting. The primary work of the conference took place in eight heterogeneous small groups. Each group had a trained facilitator(s) who helped stimulate and focus discussion, keep the group on track, and manage

---

New Baldwin Corridor Coalition
Building a Twenty-First Century Industrial Community

7:00 A.M.	Registration
7:30 A.M.	Meeting opening—Fran Cunningham, Chair, NBCC

Brief remarks
Chair, Board of Supervisors, Local Municipality
Executive Vice President, Regional Economic
    Development Agency
President, Central Regional Labor Council
Pennsylvania Commissioner of Basic Education

Brief history of the NBCC	Ike Gittlen, President, United Steelworkers of America Local 1688 Vice-Chair, NBCC
Overview of activities	Facilitator

Explanation of small group facilitator's role and guidelines/ground rules

8:15 A.M.	Small group meetings

Issue #1: The NBCC seeks to enhance the global competitiveness of new and existing enterprises along Route 230, from Harrisburg Area Community College to Penn State/ Harrisburg, and ensure well-paying jobs for our region.

Question A: From your personal perspective, what does it take to become globally competitive and create or maintain well-paying jobs for our region?

Question B: What are the competitive issues for the enterprise, institution, or organization that you represent?

9:15 A.M.	Coffee break

Figure 3.7
Program for the Strategic Planning Conference (continued)

time. By having balanced representation of various constituents in each small group, these groups comprised rough microcosms of the coalition. This design stimulated exchange of information, feelings, and views across sectors to broaden and deepen understanding and help identify common concerns among the various participants.

Figure 3.7 *(continued)*

9:30 A.M.   Small group meetings—continued

Issue #2: The NBCC was founded upon the belief that labor, government, education, the community, and business can more effectively meet the challenge of global competition and the desire to maintain and create well paying jobs through new forms of cooperation and mutual assistance.

> *Question:* How do you see these various enterprises, organizations, and institutions helping each other toward these two objectives?

10:30 A.M.   Break

10:45 A.M.   Small group meetings—continued

Issue #3: The NBCC's existence is based upon the belief that a diverse organization that is focused on the goals of global competition and the maintenance and creation of well-paying jobs can facilitate improvements toward these objectives.

> *Question A:* What should the coalition do to help your organization improve its competitive position and maintain or create well-paying jobs?

> *Question B:* What role could your organization play in making the NBCC globally competitive and maintain or create well-paying jobs?

11:50 A.M.   Break

12:00 NOON   Working lunch
             Summary of themes from small group meetings
             Next steps in coalition development
             Solicit participant involvement in future coalition activities
             Feedback on conference

1:00 P.M.   Conference adjourns

Guidelines and ground rules for the groups also helped focus participants' attention on identifying common ground for developing the network beyond its current state. I developed a proposed first set of guidelines and ground rules from general search process principles.

The design team made several changes to these. Later, discussions in SC meetings and with several facilitators led to changes based on meeting goals and professional experience. Figure 3.8 gives the set of guidelines/ground rules used at the conference. Both the heteroge-

---

Guidelines

- Activities are designed to create a shared understanding/vision of NBCC.

- Future orientation—What do we want to make happen?

- Thinking will focus on the coalition as a total system, how it links to the world at large, and how organizations function as part of the coalition.

- We'll use open sharing of information and views to explore questions.

Ground Rules

- No problem solving—awareness, understanding, and learning focus.

- All ideas are valid—there's no need to agree on responses.

- Data generated will be recorded on flip charts and then typed, reproduced, and distributed to participants at lunch. Data belong to coalition members.

- No lectures—emphasis on dialogue.

- No pleading self-interests or personal agendas.

- Only one person talks at a time.

- Task-oriented activity—need to stick to time frames, work efficiently, start and finish on time.

- Facilitators will provide general structure for tasks, help guide discussion, and manage time.

- Participants are responsible for generating data—everyone participates.

- Facilitators will recap each item on flip charts for accuracy.

Figure 3.8
Guidelines and Ground Rules for the NBCC Strategic Planning Conference

neous make-up of groups and the guidelines helped minimize the effects of power differences during small group discussions.

The sequence of issues and questions for small group discussion followed the general flow of the search process:

- *General exploration:* Statement of NBCC purpose (Issue #1)

  Question A—Nature of global competitiveness

  Question B—Competitive issues for organization
- *Nature of NBCC:* Interorganizational collaboration required (Issue #2)

  Question—How various organizations may collaborate to carry out the larger purpose of making NBCC globally competitive.
- *NBCC-individual organization interaction*

  Question A—Ways coalition can help specific organizations

  Question B—Ways organizations can contribute to coalition

In short, the sequence of work went from (1) surfacing general ideas about the nature of global competitiveness and the issues it poses for organizations, to (2) exploring ways organizations may collaborate through NBCC to make the area more globally competitive, to (3) identifying possible ways the coalition might help member organizations and ways they might contribute to reaching its goals. This flow from a highly general and abstract focus to a relatively specific concrete one reflects a key aspect of the basic search process that helps organizations create common ground for future work.

Outcomes

Participants willingly engaged in responding to questions and discussing issues and facilitators had to "call time" to end virtually all discussion periods. Facilitators wrote key discussion points on flip charts for clarity and understanding. Flip chart sheets were also used to prepare a summary of group discussions. Conference participants received a partial verbal summary of outcomes as quick feedback during the working lunch, the final session of the meeting. Data from small discussion groups were content analyzed and summarized, and a full written report was distributed to all conference participants and network members. Table 3.1 provides a summary of discussion outcomes.

Factors required for global competitiveness of region:

- Infrastructure—transportation, assistance, information, available capital

- Strategizing/planning—assessing resources, emphasize quality/value

- Education and training—educated workforce, improve at all levels

- Vision—long-term, strategic vision oriented to total community

- Collaboration—foster "we're all in it together" attitude and commitment

Competitive issues for organizations, institutions, or enterprises:

- Government—regulation, intergovernmental cooperation needed

- Taxes—tax reform, state taxes vs. other states

- Attitudes/perceptions—new ways of thinking, cooperation, risk taking

Ways for NBCC organizations, institutions, and enterprises to help each other:

- Cooperation—municipal governments, general, joint decision making, labor-management, all schools

- Communication—among all community sectors, among specific sectors

- Planning—goals, planning, and resource identification

- Attitudes/perceptions—stress common interests, members must think beyond traditional roles

- Mechanisms—bring people together, regional forum to handle conflicts, central information and referral agency

Ways for NBCC to help member organizations:

- Direct services—develop plans, provide information, conduct research and educate on "success" in other communities, conduct research on coalition organizations

- Intangible services that facilitate and promote linking many organizations, facilitate networking, focus on community spirit, and help build new relationships.

Table 3.1
Summary of NBCC Strategic Planning Conference Outcomes

The detailed report on conference outcomes served as a basis for developing a revised role statement of basic coalition functions and for developing plans for future projects and activities. It continues to provide a rich store of information for understanding, discussing, and planning many aspects of the network. Although it was unintended, a paper on the meaning of networks from a participant's perspective also resulted from the meeting (Chisholm, 1996). Analysis of data from the conference showed that participants had considerable intuitive understanding of NBCC as an interorganizational network. They also expressed keen interest in NBCC activities.

Analysis of responses to the evaluation form showed that participants were generally enthusiastic about the conference. They identified information/learning about the NBCC, the process of the meeting, the community orientation of the coalition, and social support as the most important benefits of participating in the conference.

A one-hour debriefing meeting for facilitators and conference organizers took place after the conference ended. Goals of the meeting were (1) to provide feedback on the conference from individuals directly involved in making it happen, and (2) to identify what was learned and make it part of the coalition. Examples of key points made during this meeting were as follows:

- Participants were highly motivated; they would attend future meetings.
- Members of groups were motivated and needed a "win."
- Handling conflict: How can NBCC help in situations where overcapacity and competing organizations exist in the area?
- Two components of coalition work: (1) tangible projects and (2) information sharing, catalyzing, orienting to overall vision, easing communications, and linkages among organizations.
- Decentralize way of viewing projects; form task forces and let them carry out authorized projects.

Overall, participants in the debriefing session indicated that the conference had been successful. They also felt that they had learned a great deal from their involvement.

Conclusions

This chapter covered the birth of an idea to use a search process to advance development of NBCC and followed it through application in a community strategic planning conference. Several points stand out about this experience:

- Convening the conference represented a new stage in NBCC development as an interorganizational network. Bringing almost 100 representatives from diverse organizations together and having them actively explore how to build a new industrial community was a major achievement.
- The conference demonstrated part of the coalition's unique role: providing a forum for all stakeholders to meet and collaborate on broad economic development.
- Holding the conference in late January showed much progress in a fairly short period. Elapsed time from early summer (introduction of search process concept) to the conference date was approximately eight months. At the time, though, it seemed that things were moving at a snail's pace.
- Doing much with little: designing and holding the conference occurred entirely with modest internally generated resources; there was no external funding. This fact clearly indicated members' commitment and motivation.

  Professional and staff time—member organizations or individuals willingly provided services pro bono.

  Various member organizations picked up the costs of the conference facilitator, materials, mailings, lunch and refreshments.
- Dual purpose and outcomes—Conference design attempted to (1) advance planning about the future of the community while (2) developing the coalition as an interorganizational network. Considerable progress was made on both fronts.
- Search process--Conference design rested on the basic approach and principles of search conferences. Although it represented a substantial departure from traditional search conferences, the design proved an effective way of meeting conference goals within local constraints.
- Carrying out the conference showed the complex, circuitous process of introducing an idea, having it accepted, then developing it into an event that worked in a specific situation. While the basic concept of using a search process had much to offer, it had to be carefully and substantially altered to meet the conditions surrounding the NBCC. This careful tailoring and creation work required extensive involvement of many people both inside and outside the network.

4

Second-Year Development of the Coalition

The Strategic Planning Conference described in the previous chapter marked the end of work to develop the coalition during its first year of existence. Chapter 4 traces network development a year after the conference.

First Anniversary Meeting

A general meeting and reception held in February 1993 celebrated the first year of coalition work. The event was widely publicized and covered by local press and television. A total of 100 individuals who represented various organizations and groups involved in network activities attended. The formal agenda included a review of first-year work, feedback of strategic planning meeting results, a video on the meaning of the NBCC, a look to the future, and a keynote speech by the state secretary of labor and industry. During an informal part of the program, newspaper photographers assembled various small groups of members to capture the diversity represented in the network. A feature story on the event with several photographs appeared in the Harrisburg *Patriot-News* the next day. The meeting was a general success. It advanced cohesiveness among active coalition members, helped identify and develop a sense of pride in past accomplishments, and provided information and publicity about New Baldwin in the community-at-large.

Public School District Collaboration

Work to improve the general quality of education in the community demonstrates an extension of network development concepts and coalition values and principles to a key area. The education committee has worked from the start of NBCC to foster cooperation among area educational institutions. Figure 4.1 traces development and work of that group. Representatives of Harrisburg Area Community College, public school systems, and Penn State Harrisburg comprise the committee. Improving the overall quality of education to support community economic and social development is the committee's general goal.

- Form education committee of NBCC
- Identify need for joint strategic planning
- Informal discussions with school district and vo-tech representatives
- Develop proposal to Pennsylvania Department of Education
- Action by Department of Education

  Waiver to allow joint strategic planning discussions among school districts and vo-tech schools

  Funding to support strategic planning and research
- Form School District Regional Planning Committee
- Strategic planning discussions
- Design and conduct community education survey

  Develop background information

  Design research strategy via discussions with committee

  Design survey committee review and revisions (several rounds)

  Conduct survey
- Feed back survey results to Regional Plan Committee members, school districts, NBCC, and community
- Business/education workshop
- Business survey
- Ongoing education committee work

Figure 4.1
Development and Activities of the Education Committee

Regional Planning Committee

In the fall of 1992, the Education Committee proposed that the Pennsylvania Department of Education fund research to support joint strategic planning among seven corridor school districts and two public technical schools. The proposal was innovative since existing state regulations required each district to develop an individual strategic plan periodically. Hence, funding the project required the secretary of education to issue an official waiver of this department requirement. The grant provided resources for joint discussions and planning, and a survey to collect and feed back information about the schools from the community. A School District Regional Planning Committee was formed to guide the research and strategic planning process. Teachers, administrators, and business and community representatives joined this Committee.

The committee developed a mission statement and a set of activities designed to support the overall enhancement of education quality. As Figure 4.2 indicates, the defined mission involved mobilizing area resources required to support education that prepares students to participate actively in the economic and social world of the twenty-first century. Activities identified for support of the regional planning committee included sharing educational and business resources within the region, involving business, education and the community, preparing students for the world of work and as educated citizens, and enhancing cooperation for the common good. The mission statement incorporates many New Baldwin principles and values.

Community Education Survey

Using the mission and activities statements as a guide, a local university education researcher worked with the committee to design and conduct a community education survey. This group identified seven domains for inclusion in the needs assessment questionnaire and selected specific questions to include in each domain. A random sample of over 7,000 households in the school districts received the questionnaire, and almost half of them returned usable questionnaires. Analyzing and discussing survey findings led the committee to identify six impact issues. Table 4.1 gives these issues with examples of specific actions.

Presentations of survey findings to the steering committee, member school districts, and community groups received much positive feedback. In addition, the joint work of representatives on the

New Baldwin Corridor Coalition

Business • Education • Labor • Government • Community
Working Together to Create a Better Tomorrow

**School District Regional Planning Committee
Mission**

To mobilize existing and new education/business/community resources both inside and outside the corridor to prepare students to participate actively in social and economic renewal appropriate to the world of the twenty-first century.

In order to accomplish the mission, we must support activities emphasizing the following:

- Sharing educational and business resources within Central Pennsylvania

- Participation of business, education, labor, and community

- Creating a visionary, futuristic approach

- Striving for continuous improvement

- Improving the quality of life in the region

- Overcoming barriers and building on strengths

- Preparing students to become educated citizens

- Preparing students for the world of work

- Enhancing cooperation for the common good

- Building on our diversity

- Refocusing education to match the evolving community

- Enhancing the region's desirability

- Preparing students for the changing global society

- Supporting a productive economy

- Mobilizing and utilizing new and existing technology

Figure 4.2

Mission Statement of the School District Regional Planning Committee

1. Technology

   - Share teachers/classes
   - Share training programs
   - Joint research and development projects
   - Home school/make-up work
   - Computer/fiber optic/telecommunications

2. Summer enrichment programs

   - One week/one day/pay as you go
   - Credit programs
   - Diverse locations throughout region but available to all
   - Gain business support/planning
   - Plan early (Jan.) to avoid vacation conflicts

3. Share in-service training

   - Sharing ideas for programs
   - Database of teachers and training available
   - Common school calendar
   - Use business facilities and trainers
   - Share training between schools
   - Share outside consultants
   - Share training with business
   - Share teacher trainers

4. Regional newsletter/video

   - Emphasize common positive issues
   - Summer workshops
   - Include areas where sharing occurs
   - Public relations
   - Graduate showcase
   - Video—use public channel to regional schools

5. Special interest/magnet programs

   - Collaboratively developing or challenging programs
   - Use technology to provide to all students
   - Two- to three-day workshops several times a year
   - Group problem-solving activities

Table 4.1
Impact Issues Identified by the School District Regional Planning Committee (continued)

> **Table 4.1** *(continued)*
>
> - Programs that challenge all students—programs not just for gifted or special needs students (examples: invention, stock market, amusement park, 24 math challenge)
>
> 6. Alternative schools
>
> - At-risk youth
> - Work with parents/community to be proactive

School District Regional Planning Committee built a high level of commitment to collaborating across school district boundaries and working together to improve the general quality of education in the area. Commitment to collaborating to improve overall education quality as a critical part of developing a new industrial community continues to the present. Further indicators and outcomes of this collaboration appear in Chapter 5.

Business/Education Workshop

Despite the high quality of the community needs assessment survey and positive reactions to it, two improvement areas became apparent to education committee members. These included the lack of information on the educational needs of businesses and other employers and the perceived lack of sufficient involvement of teachers' union representatives in the research process. These limitations and experience with the search process at the Strategic Planning Conference caused several members of the regional planning committee (as well as members of the steering committee) to recognize the potential of holding a meeting for teachers, administrators, labor union representatives, and business managers. Consequently, the planning committee asked me to chair a small team to design and conduct a half-day search process in June 1993.

Several design team meetings and discussions with the planning committee led to the conference design. Approximately 35 individuals participated in the business/education workshop. Workshop design used a total group meeting to welcome participants, give an overview of the history, activities, vision, and mission of New Baldwin, and orient individuals to work during the session. I facilitated the workshop. Basic work took place in four small heterogeneous groups of business, teacher, union, and school administration representatives. A trained facilitator helped each group focus on and generate responses to a set of open-ended questions. Most facilitators had also worked with a small group at the Strategic Planning Conference.

The design team developed a set of issue statements and questions that guided small group discussions. These followed search conference design by having exploration proceed from broad issues to specific organization-coalition actions. In addition, the design encouraged participants to search for ways of improving public education within the context of New Baldwin activity. The following issue statements and questions were used:

- **Issue 1:** The NBCC seeks to enhance the global competitiveness of new and existing enterprises and ensure well-paying jobs for our region.

  Question: What are the education issues involved in making organizations and institutions in the region globally competitive?

- **Issue 2:** Work at the strategic planning meeting in January 1993 identified education as a key factor in making organizations and institutions in the region globally competitive.

  Question A: What skills and abilities must individuals have to perform successfully on the job in the year 2000?

  Question B: What general attitudes, values, and basic behavior patterns will be required for employees to perform effectively on the job in the year 2000?

  Question C: What other factors will be important for employees to perform effectively in the workplace in the year 2000?

- **Issue 3:** The existence of the NBCC is based upon the belief that a diverse organization that is focused on the goals of global competition and the maintenance and creation of well-paying jobs can facilitate improvements toward these objectives.

  Question A: What should the coalition do to help your organization develop its capacity to improve employee's knowledge, skills, and attitudes to meet global competition?

  Question B: How can your organization contribute to improving the quality of employee education and development to help make the New Baldwin region globally competitive?

Outcomes of the meeting and feedback from participants indicated that the meeting succeeded in expanding and deepening the thinking of individuals who attended the event. Workshop participants identified a list of issues important to both business leaders and educators as specific meeting output. The meeting also helped strengthen identification of regional planning committee members with New Baldwin. Table 4.2 summarizes business/education workshop outcomes and reflections on the coalition–education committee relationship.

Sponsoring this event demonstrated the ability of coalition members to assess and identify ways of improving a successful ongoing activity, to relate learnings from a previous event to the activity, and to adjust plans and actions accordingly. Functioning of the education committee also indicates successful diffusion of the New Baldwin philosophy and approach to a mininetwork within the over-

---

Workshop Outcomes

- Enhanced understanding of importance of public education to broad economic development

- List of issues important to business leaders/educators

- Increased identification of regional planning committee members with NBCC

- Education survey of businesses

Reflections on New Baldwin/Education Committee

- Workshop indicates coalition capacity to learn from previous experiences and use learnings to adjust plans

- Demonstrates successful diffusion of New Baldwin network principles to a mininetwork

- Shows recognition of importance of using network principles and approach to design/plan projects and develop new mininetworks

- Reveals a strategy for New Baldwin growth: Develop increasing number of autonomous mininetworks under coalition umbrella

---

Table 4.2
Outcomes of Workshop and Reflections on New Baldwin/Education Committee

all organization.The experience helped the steering committee learn the importance of conceptualizing activities consistent with network principles and of orienting/socializing members of new committees or task forces to these principles. Recognizing the concept of having the coalition create, inculcate New Baldwin values and principles, and guide mininetworks (e.g., education) is important to continuing development of the coalition.

Business Education Survey

As a result of the workshop, the education committee concluded that greater understanding of business educational requirements was needed. Hence, the committee had a survey research specialist at Penn State Harrisburg prepare a short questionnaire from general issues identified during the workshop. This questionnaire was sent to a small set of area business organizations. Results included business managers' perceptions of the relative importance of various roles of public education. Table 4.3 indicates the strong weight these managers placed on the role of public education in providing students with fundamental reading, writing, and mathematical skills and in helping them become lifelong learners. Respondents also placed some, but considerably less emphasis on helping students develop critical thinking skills and feelings of self-worth. Managers attached little importance to having public schools directly prepare graduates for work. Managers also placed relatively little importance on helping students develop ethical judgment, preparing them to adapt to change, providing education about computers and other technology, and helping students develop skills to work collaboratively with others. The research team summarized these data in a report and distributed it to survey participants and other businesses. The education committee also has used the information to help plan future ways of strengthening public education.

Developing Goals and Projects

From September through December 1993 an expanded steering committee of 22 individuals engaged in a series of five planning workshops. These were designed to advance common understanding of the coalition role and mission and to define goals and projects for 1994–1995. The workshops extended planning work started by the Strategic Planning Conference and continued in the summer to identify specific longer-term projects and goals.

Dennis Bellafiore and I co-chaired a six-person design team that designed and planned the workshops. The two of us also facilitated workshop sessions. Dennis is an experienced manager and con-

Which item is most important for public schools to provide? N=186			
Item	**Number**	**Percentage**	**Rank**
Provide fundamental skills (e.g., reading, writing, mathematics) instruction to students	93	50.0	1
Help students become lifelong learners	19	10.2	2
Help students develop critical thinking skills	18	9.7	3
Help students develop self-worth	14	7.5	4
Help students develop individual responsibility	7	3.8	5
Work closely with business and industry to prepare graduates for work	6	3.2	6
Help students develop ethical judgment	5	2.7	7
Help students adapt to change	3	1.6	8
Provide education about computers and other technology	3	1.6	8
Help students develop skills to work collaboratively with others	2	1.1	10

Table 4.3
Top Ten Responses of Selected Businesses Ranking of Public School Purpose

sultant who joined New Baldwin during the spring of 1993. He and I have worked closely since then on designing and facilitating many NBCC events. The workshops used the process shown in Figure 4.3 to develop goals and projects for the next two years.

The series of workshops used inputs from planning work conducted earlier in the year, built upon them, and developed them into goals and project activities. Sources of inputs included a list of goals and projects submitted by several participants in the January Strategic Planning Conference and a partial list developed by several

Pre-Work

Participants receive information packet and complete the following work before the first planning meeting:

- Review assumptions about the coalition and its work.

- Review and add to list of goals members submitted earlier via survey.

- Analyze goals by answering the following questions for selecting coalition work.

  1. Is this an activity that only NBCC can do?

  2. Does NBCC have a clear and distinct advantage?

  3. Will this activity cause change in organizations, institutions, and individuals that belong to the coalition?

Workshop 1

- Orient participants, define tasks, answer questions.

- List, discuss, and clarify goals identified by participants.

- Select goals for coalition work during next year; participants allocated "votes" among identified goals

Workshops 2–5

- Distribute, review, and discuss summaries of outcomes of previous workshops.

- Define, discuss, and select goals and projects that foster progress toward goals.

- Write goal and project statements for 1994–1995

Post-Work

- Report of 1994–1995 goal and project statements.

- Use goal statements to guide coalition work during the next two years.

Figure 4.3
Design of Planning Workshops

steering committee members. Participants received a list of these, reviewed them, and added to the list before the first meeting. They also assessed the goals/projects list using coalition criteria for selecting work appropriate for the network.

Extensive discussions occurred during the workshops and often they strayed from the task at hand to direct or indirect questions and discussion about the nature of the coalition, its mission as a network organization, and its role compared with other organizations in the community. Despite such digressions, these discussions carried out work essential to development of the network. In fact, these "non-task" discussions carried out the design team's strategy for engaging members in development work on the network. Previous experience indicated that steering committee members would be unwilling to engage directly in coalition organization development work at the start of the workshops. Consequently, the design team decided to focus on the task of defining goals and projects and to use discussions that occurred spontaneously about mission, vision, and overall role to advance understanding of the nature of the coalition. For example, Dennis and I perceived a need for participants to discuss, clarify, and reach a shared understanding of the New Baldwin mission statement. However, workshop participants emphatically responded "no" when given an opportunity to review and discuss the existing mission statement early in the goal/project development process.

Despite this overt response, considerable discussion about the mission and role of the coalition took place as part of task work. We facilitated this process and recorded key comments about mission and role on a separate flip chart. This spontaneous discussion contributed to deepening shared understanding of the coalition, its role, and mission. Between workshop sessions, Dennis and I used comments from these discussions to draft a revised mission statement (see Figure 4.4). We presented this revised statement during the third planning meeting at a time when participants seemed ready to discuss the mission statement directly. Members discussed it briefly, suggested minor changes, and reviewed and adopted the new statement at the next meeting. Since then, members have demonstrated their acceptance of this statement, and, despite occasional lapses or confusion, it continues to guide coalition work.

Progress during the five workshops was slow and at times difficult and frustrating. However, at the end of the process an ambitious set of goals and projects had been defined for the next two years. Table 4.4 gives examples of goals and planned activities developed during the planning workshops.

New Baldwin Corridor Coalition
Creating a Quality Community for the Twenty-first Century

Overall Mission

To mobilize resources both inside and outside the corridor to help bring about social and economic renewal appropriate to the world of the twenty-first century.

In accomplishing this mission we place high value on:

- People
- Community
- Cooperation
- Sustainable growth
- Social and environmental responsibility

With an intent to create and support value-adding activities that:

- Are unique
- Provide distinct advantage
- Cause positive change in organizations, institutions, and individuals

Mobilization Strategies for the 1990s

- Establish a coalition of government, labor, community, business, and education leaders.

- Involve every regional institution in the creation of a prototypical twenty-first-century community that can compete globally and provide an advanced standard of living.

- Acknowledge the need for major cultural change in our institutions and ourselves.

- Prove that existing communities can convert to meet global realities.

- Focus on business revival, educational integration, human resources, governmental restructuring, housing and human services, and research and technology.

Figure 4.4
Revised Mission Statement

Economic Development

- Identify, examine, and educate community about barriers in adaptive land use.

- Work mutually with the Enterprise Zone Advisory Committee to pursue specific economic development projects.

- Continue to support and facilitate economic development in the area.

- Work to secure capital for the NBCC.

Education

- Continue to assist the school district regional planning process by:

  Reporting results of the regional needs assessment surveys to members of the NBCC and the total community.

  Supporting work on identified impact issues.

- Look for ways of helping to develop long-term linkages among key groups (e.g., business, labor, educators, parents) that have primary interest in education.

- Continue to explore the full range of educational needs and resources in the NBCC (e.g., secondary, higher education, parochial and private schools, proprietary schools, consultants, in-house educators, intern and apprenticeship programs).

Enterprise Alliance

In 1994–1995 the coalition will foster development of an enterprise alliance among selected business organizations and labor unions. The alliance will develop new forms of labor-industry cooperation to enhance enterprise competitiveness, job growth, and quality of work life. Steps involved in developing the alliance will include the following:

- Design and plan development process

- Meet with enterprise alliance steering committee; review and receive approval of plans

- Interview key managers and labor officials

Table 4.4
Examples of Goal Statements from Planning Workshops (continued)

Table 4.4 *(continued)*

- Analyze and summarize interview data
- Report findings to alliance and New Baldwin steering committees
- Define action steps
- Convene enterprise alliance meeting

Intergovernmental Cooperation

- Encourage exploration of establishing an intermunicipal government organization.
- Support corridor municipalities working to develop shared service delivery in police, waste disposal, planning, zoning, fire, and infrastructure standardization (sewage, water, etc.).
- Look at standardizing permitting—sewage, water, building permits—and the process for handling variances.

These shared goals and projects provided the basis for planning and managing coalition work during 1994–1995. For example, two proposals based on this work were prepared and submitted to potential funding agencies in January 1994. In addition, the development process used to generate the goals and projects caused increased shared understanding of the coalition role and mission among network members who participated in the sessions. The process also helped improve functioning of the steering committee.

The two proposals incorporated most of the goals and projects developed during the planning workshops. One proposal to the Pennsylvania Department of Labor and Industry covered a process for developing an "enterprise alliance" as a mininetwork organization among employing organizations and unions to identify joint approaches for dealing with key future issues facing both management and labor. This proposal received funding in late 1994. A description of work to develop this Alliance appears in Chapter 5. A larger proposal for $300,000 was developed for submission to the Pennsylvania legislature. This proposal included work to conduct action research to develop New Baldwin; identify ways of developing long-term linkages among key groups that have primary interest in education; identify barriers to adaptive land use and educate the community about them; and explore the formation of an intergovernmental organization to promote cooperation among eight municipal government units. Despite early indications of possible support, attempts to obtain funding from the legislature were unsuccessful.

Other Key Events

Several other important events occurred during 1993 that reflected NBCC work and/or had potential impacts on future activity.

Opening a New Business

The first event was the opening of a small manufacturing organization in a municipality within the New Baldwin Corridor. Although it was a small operation, the firm had considerable potential to expand and create additional jobs in the future. Setting up manufacturing in an old plant building also demonstrated the possibility of using existing facilities for new businesses. As the first new business in the corridor, the operation served as a "win" and a symbol of hope. Strong support from the staff of an economic development agency, which has been active in New Baldwin work, helped management set up the manufacturing facility and get it running.

Intermunicipal Cooperation

Another activity involved developing a proposal for a small grant to use action research to improve cooperation among the eight municipal government units in the corridor varying in size from over 52,000 inhabitants to fewer than 1,200. Increased cooperation among municipal government units had appeared as a desired goal in both the business survey and at the Strategic Planning Conference. One conference participant saw a need for "municipal government cooperation to end parochialism to increase cooperation and reduce costs."

I developed a proposal to use a small team (a project leader plus three to four graduate students) to engage municipal leaders in a process of discussion, interviews, feedback of information, planning action steps, evaluating outcomes, and planning and initiating further action. The participative action research process aimed to maximize municipal leaders' involvement during each phase of research. The proposal also included involving other stakeholders (e.g., business, citizens) in the development process. This participative approach was designed to help ensure that the process belonged to individuals most knowledgeable about the issues and most directly affected by outcomes of the process.

Although the project did not receive funding, preparing the proposal provided an opportunity to apply network development concepts to creating another mininetwork that reflected coalition values and principles. In this way, members learned about the nature of network organizations by designing the process for developing the mininetwork. As the 1994–1995 goals showed, New Baldwin continues to support efforts to increase intermunicipal collaboration. Discussion among the eight municipalities to increase joint service provision (e.g., establishing a regional police department) and cooperation (e.g., joint purchasing and training) has continued.

Recycling "Old" Industrial Sites

In July the NBCC sponsored a general community meeting on recycling "old" industrial sites. As in many other American communities, the coalition area contains many sites that have been used by one or more manufacturing firms over long periods of time. Many of these firms had production processes that used toxic chemicals or industrial processes that pose environmental risks under existing federal and state laws and regulations. Since it is often difficult to define the actual risks involved accurately, organizations cannot establish the extent of their liability. In addition, current owners may be liable for environmental hazards that existed before they acquired the property. For these reasons, organizations are often reluctant to buy an old plant site.

Based on the 1992 survey of managers and other information, the steering committee recognized this issue as important to future development and sponsored the general meeting as a forum for presenting and discussing several sides of the issue. Three experts, a lawyer with federal superfund experience, a staff member of the environmental committee of the state senate, and the economic development director of a rural county, made presentations and responded to questions. The meeting highlighted a key community economic/social development issue and helped educate coalition members and the community on several aspects of it.

Holding the meeting also raised a critical question about New Baldwin's political role: Should the coalition attempt to influence the state legislature to change existing law and regulations on the reuse of "old" industrial sites? Discussions at later steering committee meetings led to a decision that the coalition would continue to convene meetings that explore constructive ways of meeting conflicting demands about the issue but that it was inappropriate for it to attempt to influence the legislature. Raising this issue and making a decision on it helped committee members gain increased clarity about the general role and functions of the NBCC as a network organization. And, the decision thus protects the group from becoming entangled in controversial political issues that might undermine broad-based support.

Dislocated Workers' Center

In August 1993, the NBCC set up a Dislocated Workers' Center at the local steelworkers union site. At first the center provided services only to long-term unemployed United Steelworkers of America members. Individuals received counseling, on-site training for various occupations (e.g., machine operators, sales, broadcasting, health care), on-job training, and active job placement assistance. An official opening of the center in October attracted several hundred people from the coalition, the steel plant, and the community. This event provided another opportunity to inform the community about New Baldwin and demonstrate coalition work.

In early 1995 the center expanded its boundary to include the long-term unemployed in the corridor and greater Harrisburg area. Staff members worked closely with the Susquehanna Employment and Training Corporation to design and deliver needed training programs and special support services (e.g., job help to individuals who have arrest records). Due to the requirements of many current jobs, the center provided several computer courses. The existence of NBCC as a network helped members reframe their thinking about employment and training issues from an individual plant and union view to including all employees in the area.

Conclusions

A review of accomplishments during the first two years leads to several conclusions. First, a great deal was done in a relatively short period of time. Obtaining community recognition, successfully convening several major development events, and sponsoring several projects represent important impacts. Second, holding the diverse organizations and groups that belong to the coalition together around a shared vision and being able to plan and conduct work represents a notable achievement. Similarly, being able to convene various sets of organizations (e.g., schools, municipal governments, labor-management representatives) to discuss ways of collaborating indicates another crucial capacity. One prominent community political leader reflected this at a September 1992 coalition meeting by stating, "I'm proud of New Baldwin—to get school districts and municipalities together is quite an accomplishment."

Experience during 1992–1993 also shows that coalition members began to understand that systemic institutional and organizational change by all sectors of the community (e.g., business, labor, education, government) is required to develop competitive organizations. Having an overarching vision of multiorganizational collaboration to create an industrial community for the twenty-first century has provided a strong impetus for work. Many individuals demonstrated strong motivation to engage in network activities by contributing in-kind services of their organizations or performing pro-bono work.

Another conclusion concerns using various forms of action research to develop and manage New Baldwin. An action research approach is essential to foster continuous network development. It is virtually impossible to conceive of building and maintaining the network without such a process. Developing the coalition requires action research that is constantly being invented and discovered and is collaboratively managed by system members and researchers. Using this approach as a key part of the developmental process provides a continuous challenge.

5

Continuing Work to Develop the New Baldwin Corridor Coalition

As indicated in earlier chapters, by early 1994 the New Baldwin Corridor Coalition was established and operating as a network organization. This chapter will focus on key events in coalition history from January 1994 to the present. The first section covers several events that represent important types of normal coalition activities. The second deals with a challenge to the network that emerged from a member organization. Remaining sections describe events designed to develop New Baldwin as a network organization enhancing relationships with the larger community, outcomes of coalition work, and conclusions.

Continuing Coalition Work

Four events represent typical ongoing New Baldwin activity: (1) a school district regional planning meeting, (2) the organization of a children's immunization clinic, (3) a general coalition meeting, and (4) special meetings with community leaders.

School District Regional Planning Meeting

On March 10, 1994, a school district regional planning committee meeting took place in a local high school. Approximately 40 individuals attended the meeting, with ten members of the coalition steering committee among them. The meeting was well planned and managed effectively. Several aspects of the meeting reflected the close relationship between the Committee and New Baldwin:

- Printed material reflected this strong relationship. For example, the mission statement and several lists were printed on New Baldwin stationery and placed in a coalition folder for distribution to attendees.
- The committee chair emphasized the NBCC's importance in sponsoring and supporting committee work to improve the quality of education. He also stated the importance of education to broad economic development.
- The school district newsletter contained information about the coalition in each of its four issues per year.
- Coalition leaders were invited to make comments during discussion and introduce other NBCC members.

In short, the meeting demonstrated coalition success in maintaining the education committee as a mininetwork organization that embodies the vision, mission and operating principles of the total network.

Organizing a Children's Immunization Clinic

During 1994 New Baldwin served as a catalyst in establishing a children's immunization clinic in the corridor. The clinic provides free immunizations for childhood diseases (e.g., mumps, polio), hepatitis B, and influenza one morning each month on a "walk-in" basis. Establishing the clinic was a result of the combined efforts of the NBCC, the Community Action Commission (a local social action organization), and the Pennsylvania Department of Health. Work on this project illustrates the coalition role of identifying a community need, helping focus the attention of other organizations with the capacity to take action on it, and providing support to carry out action.

General Coalition Meeting

A general meeting in early August 1994 gives another example of ongoing coalition work. Communicating to the general community about the current coalition goals and projects was the primary purpose of the meeting. A second purpose involved deepening understanding of coalition members who led the meeting (particularly several new members) about the nature of New Baldwin, its philosophy and goals.

Dennis Bellafiore and I co-chaired a small team that led design and coordination work for the event. Designing the meeting involved selecting the topics and presenters, choosing a place and time, and defining guidelines for the presentations. Presentation guidelines appeared as five questions:

- Why am I involved in New Baldwin and the specific project/program I am presenting today?
- What is this program (the presentation topic) about? How is it unique?
- How can we create the future together? What are some of the coalition's leading future goals?
- What does this project/program bring to you and the community?
- How can you get involved in coalition work?

These questions aimed to broaden and deepen understanding of New Baldwin, enhance commitment to it, and encourage enthusiasm about being involved to community members.

A presentation on the NBCC vision and mission, a brief history, and the way the network organization works set the stage for later presentations. An overview of 1994–1995 goals and projects followed. Later presentations dealt with three aspects of developing the physical infrastructure of the corridor (industrial development sites; analysis of the expansion potential of key industries; establishing a business incubator). Other presentations covered education committee work, activity to develop intergovernmental cooperation, and a proposed Enterprise Alliance project.

In general, the meeting was successful. The 30 individuals who attended paid close attention to the presentations and many of them remained after the official meeting ended to ask questions and discuss coalition work. Designing and conducting the meeting also pulled steering committee members and other presenters together and provided an overview of New Baldwin and its work at the time. Media coverage, especially the TV tape broadcast several times by the public access station, also helped inform and update the general community on NBCC activities.

Special Meetings with Selected Community Leaders

Early in 1995 I had arranged with Professor Bjorn Gustavsen of the Swedish Institute for Work Life Research to meet with Penn State Harrisburg graduate students and faculty during a scheduled trip to the United States. Bjorn's two-day visit also provided an opportunity for New Baldwin to sponsor two events for different groups of community leaders. Approximately 25 leaders from state and county government, business, labor, and the community attended a breakfast presentation and discussion of the LOM project, a five-year Swedish effort to develop local and regional networks. LOM stands for "leadership, organization, and codetermination" in Swedish (Gustavsen, 1992). Later, about 30 individuals from the New Baldwin SC, New Baldwin Corridor Enterprise Zone Board, and Capital Area Labor Management Committee Board discussed this project and several other system development efforts. These events provided participants with new information about interorganizational network development work in Scandinavia. In addition, discussion helped participants see parallels between the Swedish and Norwegian experiences and work to build New Baldwin. These events demonstrated again coalition ability to convene leaders from diverse groups to engage in different ways of exploring unusual topics.

Dealing with a Challenge

A potentially serious threat to New Baldwin began to surface at a steering committee meeting early in 1994. Figure 5.1 gives the sequence of relevant events that were part of this challenge.

• Head of agency ("Sam") questions role of coalition at NBCC steering committee meeting	March 1994
• Sam writes letter that raises questions about role of NBCC in economic development	April 1994
• Sam meets with Ike and informs him that his agency intends to purchase a 65-acre site in the corridor from Bethlehem Steel	early Sept. 1994
• Agency writes letter to Bethlehem Steel offering to purchase the 65-acre parcel	early Oct. 1994
• Ike confronts Sam before New Baldwin meeting	mid-Oct. 1994
• Quiet period with much behind the scenes discussion	mid-Oct. 1994 to Nov. 1995
• New Baldwin Holding Corporation formed	Nov. 1995

Figure 5.1
Sequence of Key Events in Agency Challenge

At the March meeting, Sam (a fictitious name), the newly selected head of a member agency, raised a question about the role of
New Baldwin. Essentially he was asking "Why is NBCC needed beyond its visioning of the future function?" Although one or two
steering committee members responded briefly about the coalition
bringing a wide range of organizations together to build a strong
community, the question remained largely unanswered. However, it
served as a sign of things to come.

About two weeks later, Sam wrote a letter to Ike Gittlen that,
again, raised questions about the role of NBCC. It clearly implied
that the coalition should stay out of economic development. The letter also stated that the mayor of Harrisburg agreed with Sam's perspective on this. Steering committee members noted the letter at the
next meeting. They interpreted the letter as (1) showing a lack of understanding of the coalition role and activities, and (2) indicating a
perceived threat from New Baldwin by stating "the Mayor says so
too." The steering committee decided to take the "high road" by continuing to work to build a twenty-first-century community through
involving many different stakeholders. It refused to participate in interorganizational wrangling.

The next outward sign of difficulty appeared in early
September. At that time, Sam met with Ike to inform him that his
agency intended to take over a 65-acre site owned by Bethlehem
Steel Corporation. This shocked Ike, since the possibility of using
the Bethlehem property for redevelopment was an integral part of his
original thinking about New Baldwin. And, the Coalition had worked
through the New Baldwin Corridor Enterprise Zone (the member organization involved with developing land and physical infrastructure) to acquire the property and use it as a cornerstone for
developing new enterprises in the corridor. To make things worse,
several "ambassadors," business executives of organizations that
were members of the agency, had written letters to Bethlehem head-
quarters requesting the corporation to sell the land to the agency.
These actions angered steering committee members and raised a
question of how to respond.

The natural response was to fight. A Committee member expressed this feeling as, "I told you, you can't trust those guys—that's
the way they operate!" Members generally wanted to "go get 'em!"
Fortunately, after considerable venting of emotions and discussion,
cooler thinking prevailed and the steering committee decided to continue to follow its "high road" strategy. Recognizing that the strength
of New Baldwin comes from the community and representation by

all parties in the community, the decision was to keep moving toward its original goals.

Confronting the challenge to New Baldwin directly occurred at a meeting approximately one month later. When the agency head arrived at this meeting, Ike confronted him with "Sam, I don't know what to do with you! I'm not sure you should be part of this meeting!" Ike explained that the confrontation resulted from the letter to Bethlehem Steel and other actions that clearly indicated the agency intention to go it alone. According to Sam, the action taken was "in the best long-term interest of the community—You'll see when all is said and done." The confrontation continued for almost an hour. Toward the end, Ike demanded that Sam send a letter to Bethlehem Steel officially withdrawing the offer to purchase the 65-acre parcel of land. After offering strong resistance, Sam reluctantly agreed to write the letter.

The final incident in the challenge to the coalition was the establishment of the New Baldwin Holding Corporation in the fall of 1995. Setting up this organization to purchase and manage development of the 65-acre Bethlehem Steel site resulted from several conversations between New Baldwin leaders and the mayor of Harrisburg. New Baldwin emphasized the need to stop the infighting by supporting the formation of a new authority that would represent all stakeholders. Based on these discussions and additional information on the situation from other sources, the mayor concluded that an independent authority was required. Consequently, he convened a meeting of the relevant parties (including New Baldwin and Sam's agency), pushed hard for forming the holding company as a way of getting the various parties to work together for the welfare of greater Harrisburg, and got acceptance of the idea. The holding corporation has a seven-member board with five votes required to take action. A member of the Enterprise Zone Board chairs the authority with other stakeholders (New Baldwin, two economic development agencies, and the mayor of Harrisburg) sharing representation on the holding corporation board.

Analyzing this challenge to New Baldwin reveals several things:

- The ability to respond positively to conflict and to act according to coalition values: Throughout, the NBCC maintained a total community focus rather than adopting a "we win or else" stance.

- The ability to help bring about a community solution through forming the holding corporation: In effect, resolution of the conflict rested on exerting influence to take the issue to the larger community level.

- The limitations of New Baldwin: Even though the coalition represents all the organizations involved with broad-based economic/social development of the community, it could not by itself have resolved the conflict. Instead, NBCC stimulated a solution by alerting the mayor to the situation, encouraging him to gather information on it, and supporting his intervention for the region as a whole. Credibility of New Baldwin and the power of the mayor's office to convene a meeting and apply pressure for agreement based on a higher-level regional perspective were crucial here.

Extending Development of New Baldwin

Developing an Enterprise Alliance

In mid-1994, New Baldwin initiated a process to develop an "enterprise alliance" among a small group of organizations and labor unions in the corridor. A Pennsylvania Department of Labor and Industry grant supported this project. Basically, the idea was to bring representatives together based on the coalition vision and mission to develop over time a mininetwork to identify and work on issues of common concern. In other words, the new alliance organization brought together a different set of voluntary partners to work in new ways that resulted from the development process on problems they had selected for work. Consistent with New Baldwin, the focus was at the interorganizational problem domain level.

Figure 5.2 outlines the action research approach that guided the development process. The first two steps involved getting information and understanding of previous work that New Baldwin had done with several member organizations in 1993. This work had involved holding a meeting with several organizations and labor unions to explore the desirability of establishing some type of mininetwork to deal with important issues. Participants expressed some interest in the idea, but with no resources devoted to developing the new mininetwork organization, the effort stalled. Gaining knowledge of this previous effort through discussion with Ike and reviewing background information was essential to designing a new development process.

- Met with Ike Gittlen to review previous activities

- Reviewed background information

- Designed and planned development process (strategy and action steps)

- Reviewed proposed development process with Enterprise Alliance and NBCC steering committees

- Interviewed key managers and labor leaders in selected organizations

- Analyzed interview data

- Wrote report on development process, outcomes, and conclusions

- Discussed outcomes and conclusions with managers and labor leaders who participated in interviews; invited them to participate in Enterprise Alliance

- Presented report to New Baldwin steering committee

- Convened meeting of Enterprise Alliance members

Figure 5.2
Major Steps in Developing the Enterprise Alliance

Strategy. Dennis Bellafiore and I designed a self-development strategy—a process that encouraged participants to identify critical issues and devise joint ways of working on them. A limited number of organizations and labor unions were selected for inclusion based on their importance in developing the economy/community in the corridor (e.g., key industry; large employer) and their perceived willingness to participate. We devised a set of open-ended questions to guide interview discussions with representatives of selected organizations:

1. What are the most important issues and challenges your organization faces as it enters the final years of the twentieth century?
2. How do you see your organization addressing these issues?
3. How could other organizations be of help to you?
4. In what ways could you help other organizations?

5. Is your organization willing to participate in a network with a small number of other groups to explore ways of meeting each others' needs?

6. What infrastructure improvements will assist your organization in meeting its goals?

These questions had the dual purpose of (1) eliciting information required to develop the alliance, and (2) causing participants to begin to see issues and the role of their organization from a different perspective—one that emphasized the interconnectedness of organizations in the region and the potential benefits of working together to deal with the basic issues identified. The strategy also attempted to help build a resource base and organizational relationships for developing the corridor.

Research team members analyzed data from these interviews and summarized findings and conclusions in a written report to the funding agency. They also prepared an informal summary of the report to guide feedback discussions with each participating organizational unit. In most cases, both labor and management representatives at a particular firm participated in the feedback sessions with each organization. Feedback discussions were used to foster understanding of interview results and conclusions and to extend thinking to the next steps needed to create the Enterprise Alliance.

Conclusions. Conclusions of the study built upon interview results and projected them into the future by identifying the four broad areas shown in Table 5.1. Potential future work areas appeared as four questions to participating organizations/unions, the NBCC, and the total community. An opportunity statement for the Coalition accompanied each question.

Convening the Enterprise Alliance. In general, feedback discussions with participants were positive and identified issues that appeared to tap into important organizational issues and concerns. In fact, several participants responded enthusiastically to the findings and conclusions. As a result, most of them agreed to participate in further work to develop the alliance. External circumstances (a strike or lockout at a local plant; reorganization) prevented two organizations and the unions representing their employees from continuing to participate immediately. In the opposite direction, several other orga-

1. **Employee resources:** How does NBCC ensure that organizations in the region have a continuous supply of employees with the required knowledge, skills, attitudes, values, and capacity to grow that enable them to provide high quality products and services to customers?

   Opportunity: Help employers and area unions attain and maintain required education and skill levels.

2. **High involvement organization:** How does NBCC help employers design and manage their organizations to enable employees to make increased contributions, and produce/deliver high quality products and services?

   Opportunity: Work with interested employers and labor leaders to invent ways of developing high involvement organizations and to identify how to provide the resources required.

3. **Riding the Wave:** How does NBCC help the corridor and area organizations leverage existing and future growth/development trends and strategic regional natural advantages to contribute to economic and social development?

   Opportunity: Serve as a catalyst to bring together various stakeholders to develop a vision of greater Harrisburg as a future trade and transportation center.

4. **Labor unions of the future:** How should twenty-first-century labor unions be organized to carry out their function of representing members and also contributing to the effectiveness of the organizations that employ members?

   Opportunity: Convene employers and union leaders to explore developing new ways of working together that (a) enhance organizational effectiveness, (b) advance members' welfare, and (c) strengthen the employer-union relationship for further development.

Table 5.1
Conclusions of Enterprise Alliance Development Interview Survey

nizations learned about the alliance, expressed interest in it, and, after in-depth discussions with research team members, volunteered to participate. A total of nine labor union and management representatives from five organizations participated in the first Enterprise Alliance meeting.

Future Work. Following the general meeting of all Enterprise Alliance members, subsequent work will follow a process similar to that used to help develop the alliance as a mininetwork. The first step involves defining a specific issue for work and identifying a small cluster of organizations interested in working on it. A small self-selected cluster of stakeholders will then meet, discuss the issue, test for commitment, and define action steps. The cluster group will implement the actions defined and meet, as needed, to report on progress, devise new plans, and surface and share learnings that result from the experience. Similar small groups will form to work on other issues identified for work. Maintaining ongoing linkages to the Enterprise Alliance will be another function of the cluster groups. New Baldwin will aid the development process throughout by providing assistance in designing and facilitating events and in helping sharing information. The coalition also will help sustain the community vision and assist in ensuring that various work projects align with the network vision and mission. NBCC will foster communication among all members and with the larger community about alliance activities.

Two aspects of Enterprise Alliance work illustrate the effects of the social ecology view of networks on New Baldwin. First, organizations voluntarily bring problems or issues to the Alliance. Here, members discuss the situation to determine its scope (How many others experience it as an issue? How many are willing to work on it?) and appropriateness for collaborative work (Does the issue require multiorganizational work? Can the alliance add real value? Can organizations learn from working together?). Second, working toward solutions to problems should increase the overall capacity of the corridor, not just meet the needs of an individual organization. An example is provided by a small manufacturer who could not hire qualified tool and die makers, an occupation critical to its operation, and was thus planning to start an extremely expensive apprenticeship program for the plant. The manufacturer could have instead brought this need to an alliance meeting and explored other companies' needs to train qualified tool and die makers. Assuming sufficient interest, the alliance would have set up a small task force to study the problem and develop ways of meeting it. Task force work would center on (1) meeting the needs of employers that experienced the problem and (2) ensuring an adequate supply of qualified tool and die makers to support future expansion in the corridor. Again, Enterprise Alliance activity aims to expand the overall capacity of the area while helping individual organizations solve problems.

Reviewing Progress and Planning for the Future

At the end of 1994, the steering committee decided to start a process of assessing progress and determining goals and projects for the next year. The committee asked Dennis Bellafiore and me to lead a small team to design and manage a process to achieve these goals. Development work took place in a series of three two-hour workshops.

Workshop Design. Workshop design requested the expanded steering committee of over 20 persons to respond to a set of general open-ended questions. Stages of the process were as follows:

1. Examining the past: What were the most important accomplishments of NBCC in 1994?
2. Creating a revised vision for the total community: What describes or represents a quality community for the twenty-first century?
3. Assessing progress in creating a quality community: Where do we stand in developing the Corridor into a quality community for the twenty-first century?
4. Defining the next steps: What should we be doing during the next year to move the corridor closer to a quality community for the next century?

The process involved sharing, discussing, and reaching conclusions about meanings and next action steps.

Outcomes. Workshop participants responded enthusiastically to the first question and identified over 20 NBCC accomplishments during the previous year. Table 5.2 summarizes these achievements. Overall, responses indicated that New Baldwin members experienced making considerable progress during 1994 and had generally positive perceptions of the network. Specific tangible accomplishments appear in the top part of the table. The bottom part contains intangible outcomes based on members' subjective appraisals of Coalition work. Participants also indicated that New Baldwin had made progress in developing as a network during the previous year. In sum, the discussion of outcomes expressed considerable pride in what had been done.

The second question asked participants to describe a quality twenty-first-century community. Several responses captured a desired systemic quality for the total community: "integration," "concern for community and environment," "need to be tied into a larger

Tangible

- Establishing the coordinator role
- Starting the newsletter
- Obtaining increased funding for several projects
- Establishing "Share the trainer" school program
- Establishing the Middletown Health Clinic
- Developing a video on New Baldwin
- Completing successful "hands on" involvement with "X" company (local firm)
- Establishing school summer programs
- Completing three studies of corridor infrastructure (real estate, industrial analysis, business incubator)
- Connecting 30 people from schools via Internet

Intangible

- Commitment from many people
- Ability to maintain dialogue with diverse groups
- Partnership with school districts
- Ability of the organization (NBCC) to look at itself and how it is developing
- Local government involvement has strengthened
- Reaching a way to get things done while addressing conflict in the group
- Continued growth of new ideas
- Good marketing tool for the area
- Name recognition outside corridor
- Better sense of the organization, and its place and role
- Moving away from old issues in a positive way
- Taking ideas and turning them into real projects

Table 5.2
New Baldwin Corridor Coalition Accomplishments—1994

view," "sense of being in control of your future as a community," and "self-sustaining network, economically viable, socially cohesive, culturally progressive." Several others emphasized qualitative features, such as, "mentally and physically healthy," "fluidity," "grandparents and kids in the streets," and "respect for each other and respect for diversity." Still others focused on the emerging importance a global perspective (e.g., "being a world place;" "universal standards for judging the quality of communities").

Participants indicated their perceptions of progress by using a 1 (just getting started) to 7 (completely developed) Likert scale. Responses clustered between 2 and 3, with a mean of 2.3. In general, participants viewed this level of development as appropriate due to the size of the effort (e.g., "problems are large") and recognition of the slow pace of large-scale change (e.g., "We need to make small steps, we can't take a flying leap to get to 7"). Others gave specific improvement needs as the basis for their fairly low ratings (e.g., "need to resolve leadership"; "only a few people have the vision—the rest of us are just trying to make it from day to day"). Overall, participants were reasonably content with progress made in developing NBCC since its birth approximately three years earlier.

Assessment and planning meetings led to two types of action outcomes. First, participants developed a set of areas for action in responding to the last question ("What should we be doing during the next year to move NBCC closer to a quality community for the next century?"). Community communications, intergovernmental cooperation, public transportation, and education were identified as major future work areas. The second action outcome was the development of New Baldwin as an organization. The assessment/planning process deepened understanding of members about the nature and role of the coalition as a network organization and its hopes and goals for the future. Work also improved communication among members, reinforced the regional vision, and extended it into the future.

Strengthening Relationships with the Community

New Baldwin leaders recognized from the outset that strong community support was essential for success. Consequently, the coalition has emphasized the need for building and maintaining ties to the larger community. Holding general community meetings and the Strategic Planning Conference were ways of retaining the coalition's roots in the broad community. In addition, NBCC from the start of

1995 organized specific activities designed to enhance community relationships: publishing a newsletter, conducting an interactive community meeting, developing a video on New Baldwin, and conducting a communications survey.

Publishing a Newsletter

The Strategic Planning Conference in early 1993 identified communication as a key coalition function. Conference participants saw the need for New Baldwin to provide communications with a total community orientation. An initial SC response to this need was producing and distributing a newsletter—*The Corridor*—in the summer of 1993. Unfortunately, lack of funds made it impossible to continue publication after the first issue.

A grant from the state enabled the coalition to resume publishing in early 1995. Grant money covered the costs of distribution and of engaging a professional journalist to edit and prepare material for publication and to manage technical aspects of the process. His professional knowledge and skills greatly improved the quality of the newsletter.

The first two issues of *The Corridor* were published in February and May 1995. The coalition mailed approximately ten thousand copies to members and other key individuals and organizations in the area. The first issue reintroduced readers to the basic concept of the coalition and described outcomes of several projects, including plans for the 1995 "Kids' College," information on the free children's immunization clinic in Middletown, Enterprise Alliance work, and summaries of the three studies on Corridor physical infrastructure. The second issue included information on designation of the city of Harrisburg as a "Federal Enterprise Community," a planned outlet mall, restaurant, and park revitalization project in Harrisburg, and the work of a task force established to explore purchasing the two area airports from the state. Both issues encouraged individuals to get more information on and become involved in New Baldwin work and information to make this possible. Several people responded to these requests.

The third issue of the newsletter was published in a special weekly community section of the largest area newspaper. The goal was to reach more members of the general community for approximately the same cost and for ease of distribution. To acquaint the general public with New Baldwin, the article covered corridor location (municipalities that belong to the Coalition), the mission statement, benefits to local businesses, a short list of organizations represented, and four members' statements about the Coalition. Since early assessment of using the special newspaper section was positive, the SC decided to continue to use this medium for the newsletter. Informal feedback from the community has been positive and in late 1996 NBCC received funding from a business organization to publish future issues.

Interactive Town Meeting

Early in 1996, the SC examined the status of coalition development and determined that a general community meeting using an innovative design was needed. The steering committee asked me, Dennis, and three other members to design and plan the meeting. Our general charge was to devise a new design—one that would require attendees to become actively involved in the meeting. The purposes of the meeting were identified:

- To promote an open exchange with key members from critical parts of the community
- To communicate and demonstrate what NBCC is and how it can help foster interchange and activities among organizations
- To have representatives and organizations share information about their activities and explore ways of helping each other and the larger community through the coalition
- To give individuals an opportunity to become part of New Baldwin.

Having individuals involved in different types of coalition work and community members engage in informal open exchanges constituted the basic design principle. Figure 5.3, the invitation to the meeting, reflects several other design features that helped ensure a high level of interaction. As the letter indicates, "neighbors" were invited to share their ideas about how to improve the community, and speeches and formal presentations were prohibited. Instead, seven idea centers served as discussion locations for open-ended exchanges among community members and individuals working on projects represented at each center. Tables at each center contained copies of brief written material on projects and were arranged to encourage participants to walk around, explore the various idea centers and the general information center, and engage in conversation. The absence of chairs encouraged people to continue to move around and seek out information at different centers. Lack of formal program structure

➤ Business
➤ Community
➤ Education
➤ Government
➤ Labor
➤ Technology

Dear Neighbor:

The **New Baldwin Corridor Coalition** would like to invite you to an Interactive Town Meeting on Tuesday, March 5, 1996. Do you have an idea on how to make the community better? We want to hear from you.

Date: March 5, 1996
Time: 5:00–6:30 p.m.
Location: I.W. Abel Hall, 200 Gibson St., Steelton, PA 17113

We want your **comments and ideas** on activities in our region. **Speeches and boring presentations have been banned!** The diagram below illustrates the idea centers which will be available. Representatives from business, local government, state government, economic development agencies, higher education, and public schools who are listed in the diagram have been invited to participate in the activities. We would like to add your ideas to these discussions.

Please stop in anytime between 5:00 and 6:30 p.m. to enjoy some light refreshments and interesting conversation. If you have questions regarding this event, please call Diane Ollivier at Penn State Harrisburg, (717) 948-6178.

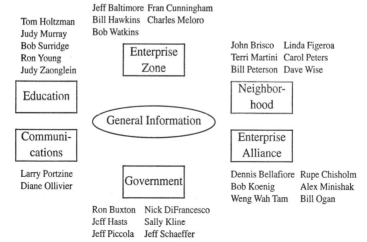

Figure 5.3
Invitation to the Interactive Town Meeting

also encouraged interaction among participants.

Observations indicated that the meeting was successful. Approximately 75 people attended, including several key members of the state legislature and state agencies, local government units, labor unions, and management. These included many "old" friends and quite a few individuals who had not been involved in earlier New Baldwin activities. Participants circulated among the idea centers, with many of them remaining actively involved in small group conversations at 7:15 p.m., well after the official 6:30 ending time of the event. One New Baldwin member observed that "It was a good format, we answered the questions they had, and impressed them with what we're doing."

A brief evaluation at the next SC meeting reinforced the positive impressions gained from observations. Several comments emphasized the high level of interaction that took place:

- "Very good idea. Wasn't as formal as past meetings, wasn't boring, and encouraged interaction."
- "Provided something for everyone."
- "We learned that we could react quickly. Instead of trying to arrange for resources, we became the resources."
- "Allowed for two-way interaction—they learned and we learned."

In short, the meeting appeared to have been quite successful and its design seemed an important contributor to that success.

Creating a Video

The idea of developing a short video to help educate the community about NBCC came up during a SC meeting in late 1994. After discussion at several meetings, the group requested the communications committee to coordinate developing a video. After exploring several possibilities, the committee arranged through WITF, the local public TV station, to use a freelance professional to produce the tape. A member organization provided funding.

The finished video became available in late May 1996. The steering committee reviewed the 14-minute tape and responded enthusiastically to it. A trial run of using the tape to reach out to various organizations and groups in the community occurred two weeks later when a steering committee member showed the video to two elected representatives of a local borough. Responses of these borough officials suggested that the video had a positive impact on them. For the first time, they seemed to recognize that some important things were happening in the corridor and that New Baldwin was playing a key role in bringing about change. In addition, these officials began to talk about becoming actively involved in coalition work as a way of making positive things happen in the borough. This experience and other feedback have indicated that the video presentation and related discussions have merit. As a result, the SC is organizing to have individual members make video presentations and conduct discussions about NBCC and its work with various municipal and other organizations in the community. These interchanges should establish and deepen two-way communication with key organizations and groups in the community. Improved understanding should contribute to greater support for the coalition and improved quality of its activities.

The Communications Survey

For several years the SC had felt a need to conduct a strategic communications survey. However, a lack of resources made this impossible until late 1996. At that time, Charles Maxwell, a graduate student at Penn State Harrisburg, became interested and proposed to conduct the survey and write it up as his MPA professional master's paper. The university strongly supported the survey by providing substantial in-kind support and a small amount of money to cover copying and mailing costs.

Charles and I devised the process described in Figure 5.4. Designing and implementing the survey followed an action research approach, and the survey included elements from strategic planning and organizational communication. The survey had three goals:

1. Assess the effectiveness of existing ways of communicating with stakeholders.
2. Discover new ways of reaching key groups, organizations, and individuals in the community.
3. Develop the coalition by using survey findings to strengthen relationships with stakeholders.

Charles worked with me and a Penn State communications specialist to develop a draft questionnaire. Feedback from the SC and suggestions from the NBCC coordinator based on her experience in producing past issues of the newsletter led to many revisions to the draft. A survey research expert also provided several useful suggestions on the content and wording of the cover letter and on the timing of the mailing. The steering committee gave final approval to the project.

The survey was completed just as this book went to press. Eighty-two of 246 individuals selected to represent coalition stake-

- Receive Steering Committee approval of survey
- Select stakeholder organizations/groups and individuals to represent each
- Design survey process and questionnaire
- Input from NBCC Coordinator regarding questionnaire
- SC review of survey process and questionnaire
- Revise questionnaire
- Conduct mail survey to collect data (two mailings)
- Analyze and summarize data
- Feed back and discuss findings with Steering Committee
- Communication Committee develops recommendations about future ways of communicating with stakeholders and general community
- Review proposed communication action steps with SC
- Implement communication action steps
- Make future changes to communications based on experience and feedback
- Use survey to advance development of New Baldwin as a network

    SC discusses meaning of results

    SC defines action steps to strengthen relationships with identified stakeholders (e.g., community groups)

    Implementation of action steps

    Assess NBCC position in larger community

    Define new action steps to develop New Baldwin–total community linkages

Figure 5.4
Communications Survey Process

holders (from business, labor, education, government, community, media groups) responded. Figure 5.5 illustrates the cover letter and Figure 5.6 the survey form used to collect data.

January 13, 1997

Dear Neighbor:

The New Baldwin Corridor Coalition has worked since 1992 to bring together various partners (business, government, labor, education, community organizations) to develop conditions that foster general economic and social development of the community.

Now we need your help in assessing our communications with the community. We hope that you will take the eight minutes required to complete the enclosed questionnaire.

The coalition is conducting a communications survey of representatives of key groups in the New Baldwin Corridor. You have been selected as a representative of one of these groups. Dr. Rupert F. Chisholm, Professor of Management at Penn State Harrisburg, is professional advisor on the project.

Individual responses will be anonymous since data will be analyzed only on a group basis. Results will be summarized and reported back to the New Baldwin steering committee. This feedback will be used by the steering committee to make communications more effective. Copies of the written report of results will be available upon request.

Please invest the eight minutes required to respond. This is the only way we can improve communications with key individuals in the community, such as you.

We shall appreciate it if you will complete and return the questionnaire by Friday, January 24th in the enclosed return envelope. If you have any questions about any aspect of the study, please contact Dr. Rupert F. Chisholm at Penn State Harrisburg at (717) 948-6052 or me at (410) 403-2332.

Sincerely,

Charles L. Maxwell
Communications Committee
New Baldwin Corridor Coalition
Penn State–Harrisburg

Figure 5.5
Cover Letter Accompanying the Communications Survey

1. How much do you know about the New Baldwin Corridor Coalition (NBCC)? (Please circle)

   Not familiar   1   2   3   4   5   6   7   Very familiar

2. How do you receive information about NBCC activities? (Please check)

   __ Friends   __ Committee meetings   __ Other

   __ Work associates   __ Newsletters

3. What kind of image comes to mind when you think of the NBCC? (Please circle a rating for each scale)

   Unfavorable   1   2   3   4   5   6   7   Favorable

   Ineffective   1   2   3   4   5   6   7   Effective

   Not understood   1   2   3   4   5   6   7   Understood

4. What would you list as the three most effective ways for NBCC to communicate with member organizations and individuals such as you?

   a. _____

   b. _____

   c. _____

5. How would you rate NBCC communication effectiveness at present?

   Ineffective   1   2   3   4   5   6   7   Effective

6. Are there any topics you would like to see New Baldwin address more? __ Yes __ No

   If yes, please explain _____

   _____

7. Are there other key organizations or groups that should be included in New Baldwin? __ Yes __ No

   If yes, please explain _____

   _____

Figure 5.6
NBCC Communications Survey (continued)

Figure 5.6 *(continued)*

8. What else would you like to know about the NBCC? _____

   _____

9. Please give any additional suggestions you may have concerning ways to improve NBCC communications. _____

   _____

10. Are you on the NBCC mailing list? __ Yes __ No

11. When was the first time you heard about New Baldwin and its activities? (Please check)

    __ In the past 3 months   __1–2 years ago   __ 4–5 year ago

    __ 3–6 months ago   __ 2–3 years ago   __Don't know

    __ 6–12 months ago   __ 3–4 years ago

13. How well could you communicate about New Baldwin activities during the last year to someone who has no knowledge of the coalition?

    Not very well   1   2   3   4   5   6   7   Very well

14. Did you know that New Baldwin has a video available?
    __ Yes __ No

    a. Have you seen the video?   __ Yes   __ No

    b. Would you like to see the video?   __ Yes   __ No

    If yes, please call *Diane Ollivier* at *717-948-6429* to have a representative of the NBCC steering committee show the video and answer questions in your organization.

15. How many of the newsletters have you seen in the past year? (January 1996 to present) ____

16. Did you see any of the newsletters in the *Patriot News*?
    __ Yes __ No

    How would you rate the newsletter layout?

    Ineffective   1   2   3   4   5   6   7   Effective

    Difficult to read 1   2   3   4   5   6   7   Easy to read

    Not informative   1   2   3   4   5   6   7   Informative

Figure 5.6 *(continued)*

17. Have you ever received a printed newsletter mailed to this address?
    __ Yes __ No

    How would you rate the printed newsletter layout?

Ineffective	1 2 3 4 5 6 7	Effective
Difficult to read	1 2 3 4 5 6 7	Easy to read
Not informative	1 2 3 4 5 6 7	Informative

18. Which do you prefer?

    __ Printed and mailed newsletter

    __ Newsletter in the *Patriot News*

Key preliminary findings indicate the following:

- Individuals report fairly high levels of knowledge about New Baldwin.
- Overall, respondents have a favorable image of the coalition. At the same time, they rate coalition effectiveness somewhat lower.
- Among all stakeholders, representatives of community groups report the lowest levels of knowledge and understanding of NBCC.
- Newsletters, committee meetings, work associates, and friends (listed in descending order) are the most important sources of information about the network.

The SC will use discussions of detailed survey results to (1) improve communications with various stakeholder organizations and groups and (2) advance development of New Baldwin as a network organization.

Outcomes of Coalition Work

There are many tangible indicators of the development of New Baldwin and of the impact the coalition has made in carrying out its work. They represent some basic accomplishments that resulted from

New Baldwin work since its birth in February 1992. Here are some details:

- Formed the coalition and started it functioning

  Held organizing meeting.

  Approved the approach, vision and mission statements of Ike Gittlen's "New Baldwin Project" proposal as the basis for developing the coalition.

  Organized six subcommittees and supported their operation.

  Held regular open general meetings and steering committee meetings.

  Designed and convened special events and special meetings.
- Sponsored and conducted a survey of business leaders.

  Communicated survey results to coalition members and the business community.

  Conducted meetings that used feedback of survey results to educate coalition members and the community about New Baldwin.
- Convened, designed, and facilitated a Strategic Planning Conference.

  Many coalition stakeholders participated.

  Results provided inputs to the New Baldwin planning process.

  Conference participants gave positive feedback on conference.

  The conference and results educated participants and the community about New Baldwin and its role in economic/social development.

  Conference discussions provided material for a published article, "On the Meaning of Networks" (Chisholm, 1996) from the members' perspective. This was unintended.
- Established an education committee and supported its continuing work for the community.

  The committee sponsored work to develop collaboration among seven independent public school districts and two vocational schools in the corridor.

  Obtained a grant from Pennsylvania Department of Education.

Obtained a waiver from the Department of Education to allow joint strategic planning among school districts.

Conducted a broad community needs assessment survey and communicated results to member schools, coalition, and community.

Maintained support for education committee initiatives— e.g., "Kids' College," learning laboratory.

- Convened and designed an Education Planning Conference.

Advanced joint planning among education stakeholders.

Outcomes were fed into an education survey of local businesses.

Survey results help inform the coalition and education committee about business priorities for education.

- Fostered cooperation among municipal governments in corridor.

Obtained resolutions from eight municipal governments pledging cooperation.

Prepared an approach for developing general intergovernmental cooperation.

Sponsored meetings among municipalities to explore and establish areas for cooperation.

- Established a Dislocated Workers' Center.
- Supported and facilitated forming a new small manufacturing firm in "old" corridor plant building.
- Helped a small manufacturing company find a new plant location that enabled it to expand inside the corridor.
- Worked with two organizations to spot a community need and establish a free walk-in immunization clinic in a member municipality.
- Conducted a process that reviewed progress in developing and reexamining the goals of the network coalition.
- Convened a general meeting on legal and environmental issues involved in reusing "old" industrial sites.
- Established role of coordinator.
- Reached membership of over 300 organizations, groups, and individuals.

- Designed, convened, and managed an interactive town meeting.
- Dealt positively with an external challenge by catalyzing formation of the New Baldwin Corridor Holding Corporation.
- Conducted action research to develop an Enterprise Alliance.
- Produced a video to use for active outreach to key organizations/groups in the corridor.
- Sponsored and conducted a communications survey.

Most of these items have been described in greater detail earlier in Chapters 2–5. Regardless, it is important to summarize them here to help assess overall progress in developing and operating New Baldwin over the first five years.

Items described briefly below include intangible outcomes of the coalition or indicators of its development. These items are things that must be inferred from direct actions taken or from reactions to New Baldwin activities. A brief review of coalition work shows the following:

- Obtained recognition in the community for identifying a crucial broad issue, focusing attention on it, and preparing and organizing a systemic approach to deal with it.
- Achieved a workable level of understanding among coalition members, its role compared with those of other organizations, and how it should be organized and managed.
- Showed the ability to bring diverse groups of people together to begin building an industrial community for the twenty-first century in a conservative area.
- Developed the capacity to convene, design, and manage events that can have significant impacts on the community (e.g., development/planning conferences, meetings, surveys and feedback) using an action research approach.
- Demonstrated the capacity to carry out much work successfully with modest outside funding. This has been achieved through substantial contributions of in-kind services and pro-bono work. These contributions, in turn, show a high level of commitment and motivation by many coalition members.

Conclusions

My experience working during the past five years to help develop New Baldwin as a network organization has led to the conclusions outlined here.

1. The network organization construct has provided a potent way of conceptualizing, planning, and taking action to develop an industrial community that meets "world class" quality standards in the next century. Including stakeholders from all key institutions, including business and government, labor, education, and community groups, helps ensure the use of a systems view of development, and, also, tends to build in ownership of the process. In addition, orienting the problem focus at the total community level enables a shared vision and mission to emerge that incorporates members' broad hopes and aspirations. Community level goals and planning are also extremely motivating for many people. Apparently, the process provides a rare opportunity for individuals to participate directly in creating a desirable future for their community.

2. Using an action research approach based on system and organization development principles provides a process for developing a quality community that can be maintained over time. The action research approach views development as an ongoing process that changes based on new events occurring in the environment and new insights from past experiences. In this way, the process helps provide up-to-date internal and external information that enable the network system to change to meet new requirements.

3. Although network organizations are difficult to understand and describe, coalition members often have shown an intuitive ability to grasp key dimensions of the system. Members tend to gravitate to the central idea that systemic institutional and organizational change by all sectors of the community is required to develop a quality community. Often, they have shown understanding of the New Baldwin role and how it differs from the roles of existing traditional organizations in the community. Members have also demonstrated motivation to engage in activities that involve all sectors of the community under the coalition umbrella.

4. The type of action research required to support New Baldwin falls toward the more open, complex, difficult to manage ends of several dimensions that a colleague and I identified several years ago from reviewing a diverse set of AR projects (Chisholm and Elden, 1993). The coalition exists somewhere between the individual organization and society levels and is a loosely organized system of voluntary members. Hence, it requires an action research process that is constantly being invented and discovered, that attempts to bring about change of key operating parameters of member organizations, and is collaboratively managed by system members and researchers. Using action research to stimulate, inform, and guide system development under such circumstances is extremely challenging. Engaging in the process is also extremely rewarding.

5. Despite many positive outcomes and considerable learning by members about interorganization networks, action research, and related concepts, several issues continue to challenge New Baldwin. Most of these flow from the basic nature of New Baldwin as an interorganizational network. The complex ephemeral quality of networks makes them extremely difficult even for members to discuss and understand. On one hand, members seem attracted to the NBCC vision/mission and understand intuitively the necessity to use a systemic approach to bring about real economic and social change in the community. In fact, during the strategic planning meeting, participants showed great understanding of network organizations. On the other hand, even experienced SC members continue to have questions about New Baldwin as an organization and its role in the community. Furthermore, since many of them reside in traditional organizations, those who are not members of the coalition have even greater trouble understanding New Baldwin, its role, and activities. Consequently, NBCC must devote considerable attention to developing effective ways to design, conduct, and evaluate its activities and to gain understanding of itself and its accomplishments among members and the larger community.

Part III

Developing a Rural Business Incubator Network

6

Early Work to Develop the Central and Northern Incubator Network

A Bolt from the Blue

In April 1993 I received a call from Gregg Lichtenstein, a complete stranger at that point. His purpose was to inquire about my interest in collaborating with him to write a network development proposal to the Center for Rural Pennsylvania. The first step would be to submit a letter of intent by May 15 indicating our plans to submit a full grant proposal on developing a network organization among 14 fourteen local business incubators scattered about the northwest region of the state.

As Gregg described it, the possibility sounded exciting. But I had a nagging feeling and wondered if this sounded almost too good to be true. So, I proceeded to get more information during the phone conversation and continued to get more details later. Information gathering focused on several questions:

- Who is Gregg, anyhow? It turned out that he had received a Ph.D. under Eric Trist and the social system science group at the University of Pennsylvania in the late 1980s. So, he was a kindred soul. He was just phasing out as research director of the National Incubator Association and was setting up his consulting firm. Part of his experience had involved developing training programs on interfirm collaboration.

- Why me? Gregg got my name from a professional colleague, whom I have known for over 20 years. Gregg had met him at a conference the year before and asked about other action research/OD colleagues in Pennsylvania. My name was mentioned and Gregg made a note of it. Gregg also revealed another very practical motive: The grant proposal had to come from a member of one of the state or state-related universities (such as Penn State). Since he was up-front about this fact, it caused no great concern.

- Is the project real? Impetus for the project came from three local incubator managers chosen in April to represent their peers. This group had the general charge of suggesting training programs and development activities for the 14 local incubator managers in the region. In addition, the regional manager of the state agency that heavily subsidized local incubators saw developing a network as a way of improving local managers' skills. So, there was some positive pressure for development, but how much came from potential network members themselves (the local incubator managers in the region) and how much from outside (the primary incubator funding agency)? This remained troubling.

- What are the expectations of the Center for Rural Pennsylvania? Having a third party fund the proposed project further complicated the situation and evaluating whether or not to become involved. The Center for Rural Pennsylvania is an independent agency funded directly by the legislature to develop policy recommendations to enhance broad economic and social welfare of rural communities. Hence, their primary interest was in receiving inputs regarding program/policy development. In addition, previous Center grants had funded traditional research based on a "researcher as expert" model—How could we reconcile this approach with a participant-centered action research development process?

- Would I like to work with Gregg? Liking each other and having compatible styles of working would be important, both personally and for the success of the project. Gregg was friendly and enthusiastic about the project. His interests and experience in developing interfirm collaboration training programs were definite positives. He had done some previous work with several of the local incubators in the region. Hence, he knew most of the managers and had general knowledge about many of the inside and outside individuals who would be key players in the network development process. So far, so good. As things turned out, Gregg and I developed an enjoyable and highly productive working relationship.

Thus began the year-long process of developing the rural business incubator network. In the next sections we'll examine the nature of business incubators, the background and early development steps of the project, the development process, and outcomes of early development work.

Business Incubators

A business incubator is an economic development program that promotes the formation of new enterprises by providing entrepreneurs with financial resources, office support services, education or training, business and technical assistance, and opportunities to meet and discuss issues among themselves. Incubators vary in the mix and scope of support services offered. They usually contain elements that separately are often found in other types of business assistance programs, such as small business development centers. The uniqueness of incubators is having these elements located in one place to create a critical mass and an organizational climate that supports developing new enterprises.

Incubators have three main objectives:

1. Increase the rate of new business formation.
2. Increase individual firm rates of expansion or development (that is, help them grow farther, faster, and more efficiently).
3. Increase firms' chances of success (or, stated differently, to decrease their rate of failure).

Incubators help entrepreneurs transform ideas into viable businesses capable of operating independently. In doing so, they provide valuable jobs, resources, and revenues to a community.

Background of the Development Project

Pennsylvania traditionally has led the nation by having the largest number of incubators as well as the most established programs. Incubators are funded through a variety of mechanisms including rental revenues and fees for services, but most require substantial state and local government support. The primary funding organization of local incubators involved in this project has been very active in stimulating and supporting local business incubators to advance regional economic development. Since 1983, it has provided over $6 million to local incubators in its region for operating costs and feasibility studies. Overall, the 14 incubators have experienced an 89 percent success rate among their tenants and an 81 percent success rate among both tenants and graduates. This effort has resulted in the creation of an estimated 2400 full time jobs.

The individual incubators in the region vary greatly in size and in the types of communities that support them. Each incubator has a board of advisors that gives general guidance and acts as liaison to the local community. Communities that surround the incubators vary from small, relatively isolated towns to a large city. Most incubators are located in small rural settings. These face special difficulties that stem from having a small entrepreneurial pool from which to draw ideas, a general lack of resources and infrastructure, and remoteness from markets.

Before the network development process began, managers of the 14 incubators had been meeting for several years at professional association conferences, such as the Pennsylvania Incubator Association, or at planning and review sessions of the principal funding source. The managers perceived each incubator primarily as a local operation responsible to its board and community. They did not view themselves as part of a larger regional set of incubators. In fact, several managers viewed other incubators in the region as competitors. Most of the incubators relied heavily on annual grants from the principal funding agency. This resulted in ambivalence by the managers toward the agency. That is, since they needed the money, receiving it caused feelings of gratitude. At the same time, the dependency led them to feel resentful about losing some control of their incubators.

As mentioned in the first section, several events converged in 1993 to trigger the network development process. First, several incubator managers began to see potential benefits that might result from building the 14 incubators into a loosely linked network. Second, the primary funding organization had come to see that building increased linkages among incubators might improve the management and operation of local units. Third, the sponsoring agency authorized funding a computer-based information system that would provide on-line communications among all incubators in the region. It also provided technical support to install the system. These events set the stage for the project, but I still had to decide whether or not to get involved in it.

Making a decision about the project involved talking with several individuals. First, I obtained enough additional information during the two weeks following the phone call from Gregg to justify submitting the letter of intent on May 15. Since the full proposal was not due until the end of August, the summer was available to do additional checking to ensure that carrying out the development process really made sense. So, I began to discuss the project with key individuals in several organizations:

- *Center for Rural Pennsylvania:* This group indicated keen interest in the project as a way of improving conditions in rural areas. They emphasized the importance of documenting progress and outcomes. (They had been burned a few years before on a project conducted by a professor at another university.)
- *Funding agency for local incubator operations:* There was strong support for the project from this group. They were interested in improving the effectiveness of local incubator operations via network development and felt that local managers could develop their capacity to have larger impacts in local economic development.
- *Local incubator managers:* Gregg made most of these contacts since he had met most of the local managers. Although they had little understanding of the project, they indicated a willingness to participate in the development process.

Gregg and I also continued discussions during the summer and began to sketch out broad outlines of a proposal. During this process, we began to feel comfortable working with each other and recognized that we had complementary interests: I was more interested in developing the network as a total system; Gregg had greater interest in improving the internal operations of local incubators. By the middle of the summer it became clear that we could work well together and that each of us would enjoy and learn from the project.

The additional contacts and discussions led us to conclude that engaging in a network development process did make sense. Nevertheless, we were far from clear about details of the development process and had considerable concern about many aspects of the proposed project. Despite the lack of clarity and our concerns, we prepared a proposal for the network development project and submitted it by the August 31 deadline. The Center for Rural Pennsylvania approved the project in November. Now, we really had to figure out what to do!

The Development Process

After being notified that we had received the grant, we began to focus on how to conduct the development process. Early work in December 1993 and January 1994 involved conceptualizing the network development process. Our discussions covered the scope of the development process and its goals, the current state of linkages among incubators, and a tentative strategy and first steps for building the network. As we thought about and discussed the project, we concluded that developing the network and reaching project goals required work at three levels:

1. *Local incubator:* Affecting managers' definition of the role and functions of incubators.
2. *Interincubator:* Building relationships among the 14 incubators and developing awareness of how individual incubator managers could collaborate.
3. *Network as system:* Develop an appreciation of the network as a total system that orients work to the external environment and supports strategic thinking about ways of improving incubation in the region.

Next, we had to decide where and how to begin. One possibility was to start at the local level and build outward. This was a tempting option since Gregg had lots of knowledge about the "best practices" of incubators. However, three factors led us away from this approach:

1. Gregg's detailed knowledge about best practices could easily lead to automatic prescriptions about what to do.
2. Incubator managers were extremely guarded about the management of their local operations, and some feelings of competition existed among them.
3. Conceptually, this would have started the development process at the wrong place. Since developing the network was the primary goal, we had to start activities at the total system level and make certain that work at the other two levels took place within this context.

Our design and planning work thus proceeded from the guiding socio-ecological perspective of developing the network as a higher-level interorganizational system.

Early Concerns

Our discussions and reflections also raised many concerns and questions:

> What was the client system and who was the contact person for it?
>
> How would researchers and members think about and refer to the network, which did not exist at that point? How could we refer to a nonexistent entity?
>
> To what extent did the 14 incubator managers feel they were part of a larger regional network of incubators?
>
> How important was participating in a regional network to local managers? Were they willing to devote the time and energy required to develop it?
>
> Would members view building the potential network as an opportunity to develop something of their own to support and enhance their regular work or merely as a formal requirement imposed from outside? Would they merely be "going through the motions?"
>
> Did developing a network really make sense in this specific situation?
>
> Would the emerging action research development process actually work? Would it create a network organization?
>
> Was there enough time to make progress toward development goals?

Early discussions between Gregg and me resulted in defining the proposed network organization as the client system. On one hand, this caused a problem, since no network existed then. But the decision was essential to keep development work from being pulled in many directions by various stakeholders. Clearly identifying the client system was important in early steering committee meetings and in responding to several later requests by outside constituent organizations for inappropriate involvement by us (e.g., a request to attend a meeting where evaluating individual incubator effectiveness took place). Discussion with the steering committee also led to a tentative name for the network: the Central and Northern Incubator

Group, or the CN Group. Answers to the remaining questions and many others that came up during the development process emerged as work progressed.

Strategy

The development strategy flowed from the guiding perspective of focusing on building the network as an overall system. Other work would occur within the context of total network development.

In short, developing the network rested on the socio-ecological view of networks described in Chapter 1. This perspective was intended to build and maintain participants' focus on the network as a whole and how it functions in its outside task environment. Using an AR process to develop the network was a second strategic base for network development. Following the general participative action research approach, developing the network involved planning, designing, and conducting a series of activities conducted jointly with members of the system. Learnings from earlier development work with the New Baldwin Corridor Coalition (described in Chapters 2–5) contributed to conceptualizing, planning, and carrying out activities to develop the CN Group. Still, many differences between the two situations forced us to rethink and invent most aspects of the development process.

The development process followed a system development approach of having incubator managers engage in a series of designed activities during the project year. Each activity or event was intended to help members move the emerging network closer to shared system development goals. Development resulted from a shared understanding of these goals, developing information on the state of the network and key features of its environment, and planning and taking action based on new shared appreciations of the situation and the network. Interventions and activities were also designed to increase members' understanding and learning about the network and its potential by participating actively in its development. Greater understanding was expected to increase network and individual incubator effectiveness.

The AR approach used required incubator managers to take an active role in the development process—by defining network goals, taking responsibility for developing the system, and participating actively in the development process. They were also to provide constant information about the realities of carrying out business incubation work in the region and implications for network development.

We formed a three-person AR team comprised of me as project director, Gregg as coresearcher, and Weng Wah Tam (Tam), a graduate student at Penn State Harrisburg, as research assistant. The primary responsibility of the team was to design and manage events that would help incubator managers learn about networks and discover how a network organization could enhance efforts to improve general economic development in the region. Specifically, the researchers designed and facilitated meetings, collected and fed back information on the network, and monitored and helped manage the overall development process. As indicated in later sections, design and planning work took place with deep involvement of the project steering committee.

Action Steps

Figure 6.1 lists the major steps involved in developing the incubator network. After early conceptualization and planning work, there were certain key steps in developing the network:

- Forming the steering committee (SC)
- Joint design and planning work with the SC
- Learning about the system by visiting each local incubator
- Holding the first development conference

Forming the Steering Committee

I learned about using a steering committee to help foster organizational change many years ago in studying sociotechnical systems. Since then, I have used these groups in organization and system development efforts whenever possible. The basic idea is to have a small group of individuals who represent various levels and functions of an organization guide the development process. A steering committee provides continuous linkage between the change process and the organization, and it helps build in ways for a system to learn how to develop itself.

From the early stages of thinking about and planning the network development process, using a steering committee to guide the project seemed important. In fact, the nonexistent nature of the network at the start of the project, the diverse set of organizations involved and their physical separation made forming a steering committee mandatory. Figure 6.2 presents an excerpt from a February 18 letter to incubator managers about the steering committee. While forming such a committee seemed essential to start devel-

Dates	Activity
Dec 1993– Dec 31, 1994	Conceptual design and planning
Jan 7, 1994	Steering committee planning meeting
Jan 7–Mar 5	Plan visits to local incubators, design interview process and questionnaire
Feb 17	Steering committee meeting
Feb 18	Steering committee letter to incubator managers on development process
Jan 7–Mar 5	Prepare for incubator visits—design entry/linking up process, arrange schedule, prepare materials, plan interviews
Mar 7–18	Research team visits incubators/data collection
Mar 21–Apr 15	Analyze data and prepare report of interview results
Apr 1–May 7	Design first development conference
May 11–13	First development conference Network development work Feedback of interview data Identify network goals Individual incubator assessment workshop
Jun 1–Sep 15	Individual incubators conduct self-analyses
Jun 17	Steering committee meeting
Jun 15–Sep 15	Network members work individually and in teams on items identified at May development conference
Aug 1–Sep 15	Design and plan second development conference

Figure 6.1
Action Steps in Developing the Central and Northern Incubator Group (continued)

Figure 6.1 *(continued)*

Dates	Activity
Sep 22–23	Second network development conference Follow-up on action items Identify and discuss learning from work to date Discuss individual incubator analysis process and outcomes Plan future CN action steps
Sep 30–Nov 23	Members and teams work on action items identified at previous meetings.
Nov 16	Steering committee meeting
Nov 16–30	Design and plan third development conference
Dec 1–2	Third network development conference Follow-up on action items Future of Central and Northern Group Complete second assessment questionnaire Evaluate network development process Future individual incubator assessment process Policy recommendations
Dec 5–15	Data analysis
Dec 16–20	Prepare report on third development conference and send to CN group members
Jan 10–31, 1995	Prepare final report to funding agency Feedback comparison of first and second network assessment findings and discuss final report with network members
Dec 1994–Ongoing	Continuing work by CN group on new action items

A Steering Committee (SC) is being formed to guide the research and actions taken during the project. The SC will consist of the three members of the Self-Directed Work Group (Jill, Joe, and Tim), Gregg, and Rupe. Another outside member may be added to the group.

The research project team (Rupe and Gregg) and SC define the CN group as the client system. The SC provides a continuous link between the project team and the incubator network. In this role, it provides two-way communications between the CN group and its members and the research project team. The SC will review research and action plans in advance. It also will help devise ways of making sure that the research process is useful to the CN group as a whole and to individual incubators. In brief, the project team and Steering Committee will work together closely in planning and carrying out the work of the project.

Figure 6.2
Description of Steering Committee from SC Letter to Incubator Managers

opment work, membership of the group was less clear. Gregg and I discussed this several times and decided to start small by meeting just with the three incubator managers selected by their peers the year before to represent them as the "self-directed work group." Our decision stemmed from considering several factors:

1. *Defining client system:* Since we had defined the network as the client system, it made sense to start tangible planning work with local incubator managers who would be members of this emergent system.

2. *Determining member perceptions:* Meeting just with incubator manager representatives would give us direct contact with the potential network system and enable us to experience their attitudes and concerns about the project. We felt that managers meeting alone with us would be more likely to express themselves openly.

3. *Gaining understanding and acceptance:* Gaining the acceptance of incubator managers would be essential to developing the network. Hence, it was important to have a forum for open discussion of the project and for testing Gregg and me: What were we like? Whose side were we on? Could we be trusted? How would we work?

Consequently, we held a first meeting on January 7, 1994 in State College, a location almost equally inconvenient for all participants.

This meeting included Gregg and me and two incubator manager representatives. The third member could not attend due to an incoming snowstorm. (Was this the real reason, or was he not really interested in the project? His later work showed him to be a staunch supporter.) Design work led to identifying several meeting goals:

- Establish trust
- Define project goals
- Identify the client system
- Discuss the research team role, the SC role, and how all participants will work together
- Discuss SC membership
- Discuss development strategy/define first general action steps
- Build SC as a working group

The meeting went very well. Incubator managers were interested in the project but at first were a bit guarded in answering questions. This changed some as the meeting progressed, especially after we indicated that the network was the client system and that the SC would control the development process. They opposed including representatives of outside stakeholders on the SC, apparently wanting to retain control of the project. At the same time, they acknowledged the importance of including information from these stakeholders in the development process. By the end of the meeting, the group had devised a general development strategy and an outline of first action steps, clarified researcher and member roles, discussed and agreed upon project goals, and had begun to form as a working group. Members had also discussed ground rules for the development process and agreed to meet again in approximately one month. By then, Gregg and I agreed to have more details about proposed action steps. In short, this meeting dealt with many issues and questions typically covered early in the entry/linking-up phase of organization and system development. Gregg and I also agreed to prepare a letter describing the development project for the steering committee to send to all incubator managers.

Second Steering Committee Meeting

The action research team took initial planning from this meeting, added details to the action plans (e.g., devising a process for visiting and collecting data from each incubator), drafted an interview questionnaire, and brought these to the February steering committee meeting for review, discussion, and modification. At this one-day meeting, participants refined plans for interview visits, revised the questionnaire and worked out the logistics and scheduling of incubator visits. They also addressed additional questions about the development process and added a representative of the primary funding agency to local incubators as a member of the committee. Incubator manager representatives readily agreed to this addition, and the new member provided valuable input during discussions. Tam also joined the group for the first time. Work during the meeting also continued the entry/linking-up process.

Incubator managers on the SC helped arrange incubator visits and devise plans for visiting several remote locations; they also informed local managers of the purpose of the meetings by phone. Approximately one week in advance, they also sent a one-page letter to all managers to outline the purpose of these visits and to describe SC activities. (This was done in response to requests from several managers.) Several phone calls also helped provide us with needed information about various local incubators.

Local Incubator Visits

Early discussions of the project raised the issue of determining the state of linkages among the 14 incubators at the beginning of the development process and establishing relationships with the managers in each location. After discussing various possibilities, we decided to use visits to each location for this dual purpose. We also designed the visits, discussions, and surveys as a first intervention. Between March 7 and 18, Tam and I visited the seven most remote local incubators and Gregg the remaining seven.

Although the responses of local managers varied, they generally showed some interest coupled with apprehension about the project. They expressed a willingness to participate in the development process but did not express enthusiasm for it. They appeared to feel that it was something they had to do that might have some positive payoffs, but they didn't have high hopes about this. Nevertheless, most of them expressed a willingness to participate.

Questionnaire. Our visits began with introductions, getting acquainted with the manager and nature of incubator operations, and a description of the purpose of our visit. After this phase of discussions and establishing rapport, we used an interview questionnaire to collect information, guide discussion, cause managers to reflect on the current state of relationships among the 14 incubators, and introduce the idea of forming a network. In short, the questionnaire and interview process were designed for both network development and data collection purposes. Our design of the development process included conducting a second survey in December in order to (1) provide information on impacts of the development process, (2) cause reflection on the state of the network, and (3) give input for further network development.

Figure 6.3 presents representative questions included in this survey. As the figure indicates, the flow of the interview went as follows:

- Identify current images of CN group.
- Define existing relationships among the 14 incubators.
- Identify state of the CN group as a network organization.
- Elicit ideas about the future potential of the network.

---

1. What things come immediately to mind when someone mentions the CN incubator group?

2. How do you view the CN group? What words would you use to describe it?

3. What would you say are the most important functions of the CN incubator group at the present time? Describe them briefly:

Relationships with Other CN Incubators

1. How knowledgeable are you about other incubators in the CN group? Would you say you understand the operations of other incubators in the group to a...(1=very low degree to 7=very high degree).

2. Suppose you faced a new situation in running your incubator. How likely is it that you would talk with the manager of another CN incubator about it? (1=extremely unlikely to 7=extremely likely).

3. Overall, how important is the CN group in helping you manage your incubator? (1=makes no difference to 7=extremely important).

Figure 6.3
Representative Items from Questionnaire on CN Incubator Network (continued)

Figure 6.3 *(continued)*

Internal Dynamics of Network

Listed below are several statements that describe how an incubator group might operate. Please indicate how accurately each statement describes what the CN group does at the present time.
Response options: 1=strongly disagree to 7=strongly agree.

1. Facilitates communications among individual incubators

2. Fosters learning among members

3. Provides opportunities for incubator managers to share their experiences and develop new ways of operating

4. Develops new ways of cooperating among members

5. Provides a safe place for discussing and exploring new ideas

6. Fosters cooperation among individual incubators

7. Develops effective ways of bringing members together

8. Helps develop pride among member incubators

External Orientation

The Central and Northern Incubator Group:

1. Helps incubator managers understand the "bigger picture" of the economy and the outside world

2. Provides information about "best practices" from other incubators outside the CN Group

3. Helps incubator managers maintain "state-of-the-art" knowledge and skills

4. Provides a broad framework for viewing individual incubator operations

Response Options: 1=very low degree to 7=very high degree

Figure 6.3 *(continued)*

Network Orientation

Goal clarity: Incubator managers have a clear understanding of CN Group goals (1=strongly disagree to 7=strongly agree)

Identity: We've all been part of groups where a feeling of solidarity or "all for one, and one for all" exists. To what extent does this feeling exist from belonging to the CN incubator group? (1=very low degree to 7=very high degree)

Holism: Which statement in the following list most accurately describes relationships among CN group incubators at present? Choose one response:

__ Individual incubators operate entirely on their own

__ Individual incubators operate on their own with a little help from other incubators

__ Individual incubators operate on their own with some help from other incubators

__ Individual incubators operate with quite a bit of help from other incubators

__ Extensive interaction among incubators occurs under the umbrella of the CN group

Future Development of Network

1. Imagine the most effective incubator group possible for a set of rural incubators. What would its key features be? Please describe each briefly.

2. In what additional ways could the CN incubator group contribute to helping rural incubators foster economic development in their communities?

3. What changes in current ways of operating would make the CN group more effective?

Using an interview to guide managers through the questionnaire encouraged managers to reflect on their responses and deepen understanding by asking follow-up questions. This technique also helped develop our relationships with the managers and gain their understanding of the development process. It also provided us with some understanding of operations of each incubator.

In general, incubator managers were cooperative about answering questions, and they discussed their local operations freely with us. Most of them were quite unclear about what the intended network would be, their role in it, and how it would benefit their local incubator. Nevertheless, they expressed a general willingness to participate in development activities.

The First Development Conference

This section covers several aspects of the first development conference in early May 1994: (1) planning the event, (2) design of the conference, and (3) actual events during the meeting.

Planning the Conference

Following the visits to local incubators, the action research team performed two tasks: (1) We analyzed and summarized data from the interview questionnaire, and (2) We designed and planned the first development conference. Tam and I conducted the data analysis and prepared a detailed report of it. Designing the conference required considerable time and thought because this event convened incubator managers for the first time as network participants.

When Gregg, Tam, and I met face-to-face to discuss the first development conference, several crucial design issues faced us:

- *Current/future focus:* How could we reconcile allowing incubator managers to create and develop their own network from scratch with the need to feed back information from the first survey. Our fear was that too much emphasis on the current state of relationships (per the interview survey) would constrain managers' ability to think about and invent a basically new system. On the other hand, we felt a need to feed back survey information early during the conference.

- *Network development/internal incubator improvement:* How could the design accommodate conducting macrodevelopment of the network as a total system and the goal of improving the effectiveness of local incubators. Would working toward one goal make it impossible to progress toward the other?

- *Creating the future:* How could we engage incubator managers with their normal emphasis on tangible, practical activities in a largely intangible process of developing the network as a conceptual system (new ways of relating among themselves, new ways of relating to the outside world, etc.)? How could we bring this "out of the clouds" and make it real for them?

After several lengthy meetings, the action research team settled on a general design for the conference, reviewed and changed it from discussions with SC members, and received SC approval.

Conference Design

The first development conference took place on May 11–13, 1994. The design called for engaging in the following sets of activities:

- *Introduction:* Personal introductions, project and conference goals, overview of conference activities, review of guidelines and ground rules.
- *Exploring general trends:* What trends in the environment will affect the U.S. economy over the next ten years?
- *Sharing views of the current situation:* What is the current status of the network? What were the results of questionnaire data collected during the March incubator visits?
- *Identifying trends affecting network:* What trends will affect the CN group as a network during the next ten years?
- *Identifying network goals:* What broad goals will the group work toward during the next year?
- *Selecting three key goals:* What strategy and action steps will be required by the next development conference?

In addition, the conference included the following work:

- Conducting a short workshop on diagnosing individual incubator operations; presenting a process to enable all managers to diagnose and assess the effectiveness of local incubators.
- Planning (preliminary) for the second development conference.
- Assessing the conference.

Activity started with an introduction, statement of general conference goals, an overview of activities, and a review of conference guidelines and ground rules. Guidelines stressed the creative, holistic, future-oriented nature of the development process. Defining ground rules helped channel participants' discussions. Using the guidelines/ground rules stemmed from experience at the New Baldwin Strategic Planning meeting described in Chapter 3.

Exploring Trends. Following search conference concepts, attendees began work by assessing future trends in the general environment that would likely affect the U.S. economy. Doing this was intended to help them see the importance of environmental forces on the network. Participants showed enthusiasm for the task and discussion of items was "alive." During the debriefing period at the end of the session, one veteran manager commented that "I usually don't like these kinds of future oriented tasks—but, I found this very interesting and stimulating." In all, they identified more than 30 trends in broad economic, political, social, technological, demographic, global issues, and environmental categories. Outcomes and discussion, which continued for several hours during the first evening, provided the context for later development work during the conference. Later in the conference managers turned their attention to trends that were expected to affect the CN group in the next 10 years. This activity encouraged managers to begin to think of the 14 incubators as a network and to link broad general trends to the network as it then existed.

Assessing Current Situation. Managers also reviewed the data collected during the March visits to the incubators. Consistent with search conference concepts, this activity was designed to introduce reality to the network development process by bringing about a shared view of the nature and current state of the system. The data showed that more than half of the incubator managers associated the CN group with another organization, such as the Pennsylvania State Incubator Association or the primary funding agency, or were confused about its identity in some other way. Managers saw the general purposes of the network as sharing and exchanging information and resources, fostering interactions among members, providing education and training for managers, and problem solving. As Figure 6.3 indicated, the questionnaire also included three sets of Likert scale items on (1) internal dynamics among incubator managers, (2) members' external orientation, and (3) their orientation to the network. Detailed results of the survey appear in the appendix to Chapter 7.

Selling Goals. Managers identified three key goals to be completed by the next development conference:

1. Developing a CN group presentation to the state board of the principal funding agency
2. Implementing the computer information system
3. Improving communication among local incubators

The managers also agreed to use the model and guidelines presented at the conference to conduct a preliminary in-depth analysis of their incubators. Despite this agreement, managers showed a lack of enthusiasm for this activity.

Toward the end of the conference, the research team introduced the idea of having the incubator managers form teams in order to improve communications and relationships, to learn new ways of working together regularly, to establish collaborative norms, and to model inter-incubator activity. Teams might also provide help in analyzing local incubator operations and other defined asks. The notion was to have each team function as a "mininetwork" that would operate between development conferences. These mininetworks would support managers as they carried out defined action steps and help maintain the network orientation (i.e., help managers get beyond normal pressures to focus only on immediate tasks at hand). Managers thought this was a good idea and formed three teams, each with a maximum of five members and grouped by geographic proximity.

Conclusion: Progress at the End of the First Development Conference

By the end of the first conference, the research team felt that a viable foundation had been established for the development process and members of the steering committee shared this view. Key accomplishments included the following:

- Developing a cohesive, well-functioning action research team
- Selecting members, clarifying roles and goals, and forming the steering committee
- Developing positive relationships and collaborative ways of working between the action research team and the steering committee
- Developing an approach, strategy, and general action steps for the development process

- Establishing relationships with incubator managers, visiting each incubator, and collecting information on the incubator network
- Establishing a pattern of working collaboratively with network members and the network as a whole
- Designing the first development conference
- Convening the network at the first development conference

These accomplishments established the patterns of relationships and defined the parameters of work for later stages of the network development process.

7

Continuing Work to Develop the Central and Northern Incubator Network

This chapter covers network development activities between the middle of May and the end of 1994. Actually, as Figure 6.1 indicated, several events carried over into 1995. Since the patterns of relationships among the action research team, the steering committee, and the incubator managers had been established, less space is devoted in this chapter to describing the rationale for our actions. I hope that by now readers have an understanding of our general approach, strategy, and ways of working with the system.

Steering Committee Meeting

A steering committee meeting in mid-June started development work of the second phase. The purpose of this meeting was to review work done so far, to assess progress toward general project goals, to capture learnings that had occurred, and to plan future work to advance developing the network organization. Holding the meeting and its design rested on the action research approach of the development process. Since the meeting occurred midway in the project year, it provided a timely opportunity to design future interventions and adjust already planned activities. Based on a SC decision, a representative of a second external stakeholder organization, the Center for Rural Pennsylvania that funded the development work, joined the committee at this meeting. Research team members designed the meeting with input from SC members. Specific work during the meeting involved the following:

- Review general project goals.
- Review development work conducted to date.
- Assess development progress.
- Discuss work required to follow through on CN group work goals and action plans identified at the first development conference.
- Plan the second development conference.
- Discuss other issues.
- Identify what has been learned from the development process.

Discussion was lively and participants readily engaged in sharing ideas and perceptions. Before the meeting, I had some reservations about having a representative of the agency funding the development project on the SC. (Would he have a traditional research view and attempt to dabble in the development process we had worked out with the SC?) This concern turned out to be unfounded. In fact, he demonstrated strong support for what we were doing and made several useful suggestions about ways of increasing support for the network from outside organizations. He continued to be an active, supportive SC member during the rest of the project.

Committee members indicated that much had been learned from involvement in developing the network. This included recognizing that there is a need for the network, that there is more to do (despite the fact that some network development work has been done), that the role of the CN group is to function as an action organization ("we can be a powerful group"), and that the work can be best accomplished by working as a group versus working as individuals. Another comment indicated that members experienced a qualitative change in "how we related to each other at the end of the first development meeting." Overall, members voiced enthusiasm for the network and its development.

Second Development Conference

The second development conference took place on September 22 and 23. Planning work conducted at the June steering committee meeting, information on the network from the self-directed work group, and information from research team member-incubator manager contacts provided inputs for the conference design. Consistent with the established pattern, the SC discussed and agreed to the design and plans for the meeting. Twelve managers participated in the session.

The meeting included the following major activities:

- Introduce three new group members.
- Review previous development work.
- Follow-up on and discuss progress toward goals from the first development meeting:
  State board presentation
  Status of computer system implementation
  Communications
- Review individual incubator experience with self-diagnosis of operations:
  Share incubator experiences with self-diagnoses
  Identify what has been learned from the experience
  Suggest ways of improving the process
- Discuss ways of measuring the overall effectiveness of local incubators.
- Review the status of developing the Central and Northern Group as a network.
- Plan the third development conference (preliminary).
- Assess the conference.

The meeting began by introducing three members who had not participated in the first development meeting. A brief review of earlier activities provided background information for new members and reinforced the importance of the network development process. Review and in-depth discussion of action items from the first development conference took place next.

Presentation to State Board

Group members were extremely proud of their experience in developing a presentation for the state board of the primary funding agency. The approximately 35 persons who attended the September 8 presentation included all incubator managers, many local incubator board members, and the state board. Since early June, members had worked as a group, individually, within their teams, and in pairs to develop the multimedia presentation. They also had enlisted production help from a local technology center in the region.

Feedback from state board members was positive. Discussion of the experience indicated that individuals learned several things from their involvement. For example, one person stated that "there is strength in numbers—we impressed them by the size of our group." Others identified the importance of working together as a total group to produce the presentation. CN group members expressed surprise at board members' low level of knowledge about incubation and concluded that they needed to become active in continuously educating and providing information to their local boards and the state board—"We need to be in there pitching with the new (state) administration." This comment reflected the upcoming election for governor and legislators in November. The group also acknowledged the importance and potential of using similar presentations with other critical outside organizations and groups.

Building on this insight, we helped managers identify other groups that could affect the future of incubation in the state. Discussion extended their awareness of the importance of external organizations/groups to the future success of local incubators and the network. Managers identified several additional stakeholders for contact and education about the importance of incubators for economic development. These included local legislators, a gubernatorial candidate, the state commerce department, and the state economic development association. Planning to contact these individuals represented a new type of activity for the network.

Computer Information System

Discussion focusing on the new computer information system revealed that it was operating in some places and that a "user friendly" expert was helpful in working out "bugs" in the system. Incubator managers identified several barriers to making the system operational (e.g., personnel turnover, time required to learn the system, and standardizing inputs). Two managers responded to this need by forming a task force to develop recommendations on standardizing input data. Participants also raised questions about maintaining the system over time ("Can we maintain the system for just 14 CN group members?") After members responded negatively to this question, they immediately began to search for ways to broaden system usage and to obtain funding.

Discussion of progress toward improved communications among CN incubators revealed that members had become less concerned about this issue. Managers indicated that the new computer system was helping them keep in touch. For example, they stated that the system "enhances communications" and "increases options." Members also mentioned the continuing importance of phone conversations ("the computer system won't replace the phone") and meetings such as group development conferences and the Pennsylvania State Incubator Association meetings in improving communications. Overall, participants expressed satisfaction and a sense of pride in enhanced communications among members.

Local Incubator Operations

Managers worked in the three mininetwork teams to share their experiences in diagnosing local incubator operations. Two questions guided team discussions:

1. What practices does your incubator carry out most effectively?
2. What client needs are most difficult for your incubator to meet?

Managers listed over 30 "most effective" practices, including providing low cost space, referrals, making connections/matchmaking, financing, and business planning. They identified approximately 20 items as "most difficult" to meet client needs, among them foreign trade expertise, industry knowledge, finding available working capital, legal problems between tenants, and affordability of transportation.

Two additional questions attempted to deepen participants' understanding. In the first, managers were asked about what was learned from the process of diagnosing their individual incubator operations. Replies indicated that the process was useful in learning new practices from others and in defining what services local incubators should offer. Members concluded that the process was especially valuable for new incubator managers. The second question asked managers how they demonstrate the effectiveness of their incubator operations. The varied responses included late rent payments, questionnaire responses, review meetings with individual or groups of clients, jointly established tenant-manager annual goals. Managers also expressed a need to collaborate further to develop new ways of measuring incubators' effectiveness.

Based on experience since the first development conference, members decided to reorganize into two work teams, and named themselves the Green and Plaid teams. These new mininetworks have seven members each. Individuals felt that such groupings were more natural than the previous three-team format. Team members agreed to work on several items (e.g., funding, identifying "best practices") and to discuss these topics at the next Pennsylvania Incubator Association meeting in November.

State of the Network

Observations from direct involvement in the second development conference led to several conclusions about the state of the CN group as an interorganizational network at the end of the meeting:

- Local incubator managers had increased their contacts with each other and were enjoying the increased interaction.
- Managers had worked together for the first time to plan and carry out a difficult and important task—developing a multimedia presentation to the state board of a primary source of financial support. Working collaboratively on this task (1) advanced cohesiveness of the group and (2) indicated a new level of network development.
- Network members had begun to work on improving relationships with a growing number of key individuals, groups, and organizations outside the network. This activity led them to understand and value such linkages and stimulated interest in developing further external relationships.
- Members had a much clearer understanding of the network. They also had developed a level of trust that fostered more open discussion of topics.
- After showing great reluctance to evaluate the effectiveness of their local incubators, managers began to engage in discussions about several aspects of the topic.
- Managers showed a willingness to experiment by working in three teams on several complex issues between development conferences. They also showed the capacity to adjust based on experience by changing from three teams to two.

Presentation on CN Group

The November 16 presentation on the Central and Northern Incubator Group at the Penn State Downtown Center near the state capitol in Harrisburg was an opportunity to inform members of state government and the community about the project. Preparing for the presentation also provided another chance for the research team and the steering committee to work together in reviewing and reflecting on work done so far. The research team described the general goals, strategy, action steps, and outcomes of the development process so far. Three incubator managers gave a multimedia presentation on the group and its work. An open question-answer period followed. After the presentation, the steering committee met to assess progress in developing the network and to plan the third development conference.

Third Development Conference

The third development conference represented a last chance to work directly with members to develop the network system. Review and discussion with the SC led to adopting the following general goals for this meeting:

- Internalize what was learned from the process of building the network.
- Deepen and reinforce members' understanding of the CN group as an interorganizational network.
- Develop concern for the future by identifying plans and actions.

All fourteen local incubator managers participated in the third development conference that took place on December 1 and 2, 1994. Work during the conference involved the following:

- Review progress on action items from the September development meeting.
- Discuss future group actions to foster incubation.
  Extending linkages to other incubators in the state
  Dealing with the new postelection political situation
- Discuss future development of the network: What is required to continue development? How will network development continue after current funding ends on December 31?
- Evaluate the process of developing the incubator network.
- Identify criteria and questions for evaluating proposals for new business incubators; discuss ways for group members to conduct individual diagnoses and assist each other in improving incubator effectiveness.
- Identify state policies and programs that will assist the future ability of incubators to support economic development.

- Generate feedback on impacts of the development process.
- Complete questionnaires on the current state of the CN group.

Progress on Action Items

Conference work began with a review of progress on action items from the second development meeting. Each team reported on activities and progress on action items. The Plaid Team reported on its activity at the recent state economic development conference and contacts with several key political figures, including a U.S. congressman, a U.S. senator-elect, and a gubernatorial candidate. Another U.S. congressman had visited a member incubator and helped it obtain funding. The Green Team described its work in developing possible options for the future funding of the new computer system and in identifying possible topics for incubator managers continuing education. Green Team members also made several recommendations regarding future CN group goals and ways of coordinating group work with that of other state economic development organizations.

Extending Incubation Work

Further discussion led to considering actions required to extend incubation work in the state. Managers voiced strong concerns about the existence of several pseudo-incubators—organizations called "incubators" that do not offer real incubator services to clients. Discussions led to participants concluding that the CN Group should initiate action on this by creating a professional certification process for (1) incubator managers and (2) local incubator organizations. Members concluded that this would improve the role of incubators in economic development, provide a way of linking with incubators in other regions of the state, and show continuing CN group leadership in the state and the nation. Each team agreed to use brainstorming to do the following:

- Identify certification criteria.
- Define the certification process—steps required to become certified and identify the agency to conduct certification.
- State other certification issues requiring attention; teams agreed to complete the first phase of work and exchange ideas by mid-March 1995.

Managers also expressed a need to reach out to the 30-plus other incubators in Pennsylvania to help improve the quality of incubation services. They identified the state incubator association as a way to reach and educate managers outside the CN group. Group members agreed to design a short phone survey questionnaire of local incubators around the state. Tentative areas for coverage in the questionnaire included local incubator needs, ways the Pennsylvania Incubator Association might meet these needs, barriers to participating in professional meetings, and possible benefits from linking into the CN group computer information system. CN group members agreed to develop the questionnaire and to request Pennsylvania Incubator Association board members to conduct the telephone survey.

Future Network Development

Future development of the network was the next topic for discussion. Managers identified the group as a catalyst for incubation in the state and stated that without the group the Pennsylvania Incubator Association would cease to exist. They also expressed a strong need to maintain the CN group and identified several requirements to maintain the network in the future:

- Regular meetings
- Facilitation (internal or external)
- Shared goals and work plan
- Funding (outside and internal)
- Commitment of members

During the next phase of the conference, participants evaluated the network development process. A description of the evaluation process and results appear later in this chapter.

Local Incubator Evaluation Criteria

The next activity required managers to consider their local incubators from the perspective of a key external stakeholder, the Pennsylvania Department of Commerce. Conference design used the following situation to stimulate discussion and identification of effectiveness criteria.

> You are a team of evaluators from various sections of the state department of commerce whose job is to review proposals from existing economic incubators across the state. There are only enough funds for two incubators. You must choose the two with the highest probability for success. How will you decide? Specify your criteria, your ranking, and what evidence you need to choose the two incubators that deserve funding.

Participants worked in two small groups to analyze the situation and come up with evaluation criteria and questions to elicit relevant information. Each small group then presented its lists of items to the total group. The criteria identified included the following:

- Impact on the community—jobs per amount invested, tax revenue generated
- Local commitment to the project (e.g., matching funds)
- Previous project success (e.g., number of jobs created, graduates)
- Financial stability
- Expertise
- Other private sector incubation projects in the community.

Participants discussed the criteria and questions and how they might apply them to their local incubators. Final work on this topic focused on identifying state policies and programs that would enable incubators to support future economic development. Outcomes of this process were included in the final report to the research funding agency and provided one set of inputs for possible state policies and programs to support incubators.

Outcomes of Network Development Process

The network development process for the CN group was evaluated on the basis of three sets of information:

1. A comparison of the results of the March and December questionnaires.
2. Findings from directly assessing the development process at the third development conference. This provided qualitative information on how members experienced the process of developing the incubator network and their perceptions of outcomes.
3. Direct observation of critical incidents and the total development process. Summaries of outcomes follow. Detailed questionnaire findings appear in the appendix at the end of this chapter.

Questionnaire Findings

As indicated in Chapter 6, the questionnaire used during the March visits to incubators and at the December development conference contained both open-ended and Likert scale questions. Using the questionnaire served two purposes:

1. It caused managers to reflect on the nature of existing relationships among incubators and to think creatively about ways a network organization could foster business incubation locally and throughout the region.
2. It systematically collected data about managers' perceptions of the state of the network before and after development work. Feedback and action planning based on survey information should also trigger and support further network development activity.

A comparison of the two sets of questionnaire results produced the following findings. (The appendix to this chapter gives detailed findings.)

Purpose, Image, and Functions of Network. Answers to open-ended questions about the purpose, image of, and functions of the CN group showed that managers greatly increased their understanding about the identity and role of the network. While most managers confused the CN group with another organization in March, none did in December. They also saw the network more as a system that could make a difference, strategically, in advancing incubation to support economic development.

Responses regarding key group functions indicated a clear shift toward activities that improve the incubation industry as a whole. A large increase in comments regarding strategic development also made this change apparent (e.g., "develop future incubator program agenda," "provide policy and direction of area incubation program"). Other responses on acting as a resource show a qualitative shift in thinking toward serving as a supporter of developing improved professional incubation practices (e.g., "building professional network," "working to develop new incubation techniques").

Internal Features of Network. Before-after questionnaire responses show that virtually all measures of the internal dynamics among the 14 incubators improved between March and December 1994. The increased role of the network in facilitating communications was especially large. Relatively large increases also occurred on three other dimensions of interincubator relationships: fosters learning among members; provides opportunities for incubator managers to share their experiences and develop new ways of operating; develops new ways of cooperating among members.

External Orientation. Three items that measured the external orientation of members showed the largest increases among all Likert scale questions. The largest change took place regarding the network helping members achieve increased understanding of the economy and outside world. Members also increasingly saw the network providing information about "best practices" from outside the CN group and in helping managers maintain "state-of-the-art" knowledge/skills.

Members' understanding of CN group goals also increased substantially during the development process. In addition, managers moved toward experiencing the network as an organization that provides a context that helps orient and guide internal relationships among incubators and external linkages to the larger environment.

Assessing the Network Development Process

For the third development conference, the steering committee decided that it was important to include a process to assess how members experienced work done to develop the network. This decision was based on a recommendation from the research team. Our thinking was that the assessment would raise awareness of important aspects of the development process, increase understanding of what had taken place, and help incorporate this learning in the network. Hence, I developed a process for reflecting on the development process itself.

Goals of the process were to stimulate reflection, capture learning themes, instill learning in the system, and provide qualitative information about what developing the network organization meant to participants. Figure 7.1 lists questions used to elicit responses about the network development process.

Managers completed the questionnaire individually on their own time. Later, members shared their responses by listing them on flip chart sheets under each question. I facilitated group discussion of these responses, and discussion continued until members exhausted each topic. Members readily engaged in discussing responses and enjoyed having an opportunity to review the development process. After the conference, the research team content analyzed individual written responses, grouped comments in the emergent categories, and summarized the data. Network members received written results of the analysis in the conference report.

1. Please think back to the period just before the interview visit to your incubator last March. What were your perceptions, feelings, and expectations about network development at that time? Describe briefly.

2. At present, what are your perceptions, feelings, and expectations about network development (based on work done during 1994)?

3. What are the key positive outcomes of the network development process for your incubator?

   Any negative outcomes? If so, please describe briefly.

4. What are the positive outcomes of network development for economic development in the area covered by the CN group?

   Any negative outcomes? Please describe.

5. Has the network development process contributed to incubator/economic development outside the area of the CN group (e.g., other areas of the state)?

   Yes __   No __

   If "yes," please describe how.

6. What learning has resulted from participating in CN network development activities?

7. Are there any other comments, positive or negative, that you wish to make about the CN network development process?

Figure 7.1
Questions Included in the Network Development Process Assessment Questionnaire

Overall, responses to questions about the process of developing the CN group showed much positive change. Before the project, managers lacked clarity about the purpose and nature of the network ("uncertain about purpose and worth") and were cautious or indifferent about expectations ("just one more nonsense project that would never be carried out"). There was also some initial skepticism and suspicion about sponsorship of the development effort ("thought it was a good idea. Unsure about who was behind effort"). General findings of confusion and lack of clarity about the network are consistent with questionnaire responses reported earlier.

Responses to the second question about current perceptions, feelings, and expectations about network development indicated a sharp contrast to members' reactions before the development process began. Group members stated that they recognize the current worth of the network, its future potential, and had increased clarity about the nature and role of the network.

Questions also asked about impacts of the development process on incubation at three levels: (1) local, (2) regional, and (3) beyond the CN region. Managers identified three types of positive outcomes from the network development process for individual incubators: (1) education, (2) stronger relationships among incubator managers, and (3) development of the computer information system. Participants expressed that they had broadened their understanding of how other organizations could help them and also gained knowledge and information to use in helping tenants. Members also experienced being more fully integrated into the network and stated that this enhances information sharing and giving support. No negative outcomes were mentioned.

One set of responses about positive outcomes for the Central and Northern region—"greater professionalism," "closer networking," "better internal management practices"—is similar to those to the previous question. In addition several participants saw the network as the advocate for state business incubators ("Our incubator group became and remains the 'voice' of small business incubators in the state"). Similarly, almost half the members indicated that the network development process had contributed to incubator/economic development in other parts of the state. Several comments demonstrated this perception:

- "Serving as the principal driving force within the state incubator association."
- "Modeling a more aggressive approach for other incubator groups to follow."
- "Increasing awareness of the role of incubation in economic development."

Understanding the importance of the network comprised the most important learning for members. Individuals expressed that they share a common fate and face similar problems. They also saw the incubator group as having the capacity to influence future funding of state incubators. Managers stated a strong belief in the importance of the network by indicating a desire to continue working to develop it. Members had experienced success by participating in the development process and expected further positive outcomes from future efforts.

Observations

Observing events provided a third way of understanding and assessing the development process. One observation deals with network identity.

Increased Network Identity. Questionnaire findings showed that initially much confusion and ambiguity existed in members' minds about the network. Discussion at the first development conference clearly demonstrated this phenomenon. At the start of activities, individuals had difficulty talking about the network and confused it with several other groups or organizations, such as the Pennsylvania Incubator Association. In fact, for the first day and a half of the conference, participants openly refused to call the network by name, despite the difficulty this caused during discussions. They felt that using a name would isolate the CN group from other incubator groups in the state. Absent a name, I dubbed it the "no name group" to enable us to carry out discussions about the network. By the third day, however, members began to use "Central and Northern Incubator Group" or "CN group" spontaneously. Using the name emerged naturally and its spontaneous adoption made a conscious decision about it unnecessary. By the third conference, members used the term freely and had begun to express a sense of pride in the group and its activities. And, their actions showed increased understanding of network identity and purpose.

Development Through Shared Task. Developing and making the multimedia presentation to the state board of the primary funding organization was a key event in developing the network. Successful completion and its meaning to members also tells much about development progress. Members generated the idea of developing the presentation during the first conference due to concern about state board members' misconceptions about incubators. Since these misconceptions posed a potential threat to future financial support, the CN group saw the presentation as a proactive way of educating and influencing a critical stakeholder organization. An earlier section described the extensive interaction among managers required to develop the presentation and the positive feedback it received.

Working on the presentation also had a major impact on network members. An in-depth debriefing at the September development conference indicated that members were elated by succeeding in a "difficult, important task." One member's statement that "this is the first time we really had to pull together to do something for all of us" captured the general feeling. Developing and delivering the presentation was important in building the network organization through members engaging in a shared real-life activity to influence a key organization in the external environment. It also symbolized a new stage in the development of the CN group.

Growing Proactivity. Observation also revealed that network members became increasingly proactive in developing plans to influence a growing number of critical outside organizations during the development process. The previous paragraph described the group's first activity of this type. Work at the second development conference extended plans for actively engaging key task environment groups to several additional individuals, groups, and organizations. These included the state economic development association; a gubernatorial candidate; state department of commerce; and key state legislators. In addition, a growing feeling of the importance of expanding to influence stakeholders occurred at the meeting.

At the December development meeting, members reviewed experiences in linking to key constituent groups, developed new action steps, and expanded their focus to include other state business incubators in the state beyond the CN region. The Group's plans to develop certification processes for local incubator managers and local incubator organizations illustrate this expanding role. Since these would be the first professional certification processes in the United States, in effect, the network, expanded its target to influencing business incubation nationally. Several other comments at the December meeting also reflected members' perceptions of the network as both a national and state leader in incubation. In brief, as the network development process progressed, CN group members extended work to include a larger number of task environment constituents and expanded the scope of thinking to include the state and the United States as a whole.

Conclusions

The planned intervention process had substantial impact in developing a set of widely dispersed autonomous local economic incubators into a network organization. Network development work resulted in relative clarity about the nature and role of the network. Over time, members came to experience the importance of the CN group to local work and to incubation activities that support economic development in the region and state. Member perceptions changed from "What are we? Do we need (want) to exist?" to "We do exist as a network that provides benefits for our own incubators and for general economic development in the region." Members also began to believe that the network has an expanding leadership role in fostering and promoting business incubation in the state and, possibly, the nation. Considering that the progress made occurred within a year makes these outcomes even more impressive. In fact, Gregg, Tam, and I were pleasantly surprised at how much development took place in a relatively short time.

The network organization construct provided a useful and potent way of thinking about, planning, and developing identity and concerted activity among a group of independent organizations. The construct emphasized the importance of the network as an umbrella system that evokes a higher-level purpose and enables members to conceive of and carry out things together that they cannot do separately. By emphasizing the importance of key stakeholders in the external environment, the approach provided a basis for having members actively engage in strategic work. Focusing outwardly also contributed to improved internal relationships among members.

Experience also indicates the importance of incorporating organization and system development concepts and principles in the process of building the network organization. While the socio-ecological perspective of network organizations provided the general framework for developing the system, AR guided the development process. Other organization development concepts and principles guided many aspects of the actual intervention process. For example, early questions about client system identification and establishing a clear contact point between the client system and action researchers came directly from established OD principles. Creating a steering committee to provide structure and process for joint decision making throughout network development stemmed from sociotechnical systems thinking. Development work also involved identifying project goals, increasing understanding of actively engaging key stakeholders to support incubators, and carrying out and assessing several action steps.

Using an action research approach was essential to the progress made in developing the CN group as a network system. The complexity of the system and rapidly changing nature of phenomena that affect its development called for a flexible approach to building the network. Using AR that called for repeated cycles of diagnosing, planning, implementing, assessing outcomes, and planning anew provided the information and experiences required to make changes based on existing system conditions. The action research approach also helped build learning from the process of developing the network into the system and contributed to empowering network members.

7

Appendix

What would you say the general purpose of the Central and Northern Incubator Group is?	First Questionnaire	Second Questionnaire
Sharing/exchanging resources	8	3
Interaction among members	6	0
Education and training	5	1
Problem solving	5	2
Funding	4	0
Strategic development	0	4

Table 7.1
Purpose of Central and Northern Incubator Group

What things come immediately to mind when someone mentions the Central and Northern Incubator Group?	First Questionnaire	Second Questionnaire
Identify with another organization, (e.g., State Incubator Association)	9	0
Lack of clarity	8	0
Relaxed group	5	2
Good people	4	1
Cooperative with common goal	3	7
Broad picture and diversity	3	0
Future development	2	0

Table 7.2
Images of Central and Northern Incubator Group

Item	First Question-naire Mean	Second Question-naire Mean	Difference
The Incubator Group:			
Facilitates communications among individual incubators	5.23	5.96	0.73
Fosters learning among members	4.92	5.48	0.56
Provides opportunities for incubator managers to share their experiences and develop new ways of operating	5.85	6.21	0.36
Develops new ways of cooperating among members	5.15	5.46	0.31
Provides a safe place for discussing and exploring new ideas	6.08	6.28	0.20
Fosters cooperation among individual incubators	5.62	5.79	0.17
Develops effective ways of bringing members together	5.62	5.79	0.17
Helps develop pride among member incubators	5.31	4.78	−0.53
Response options: 1 = strongly disagree to 7 = strongly agree			

Table 7.3
Internal Dynamics of the Central and Northern Incubator Group

Item	First Questionnaire Mean	Second Questionnaire Mean	Difference
The Incubator Group:			
Helps incubator managers understand the "bigger picture" of the economy and the outside world	2.85	4.88	2.03
Provides information about "best practices" from other incubators outside the CN group	3.77	5.20	1.43
Helps incubator managers maintain "state-of-the-art" knowledge and skills	4.54	5.37	0.83
Provides a broad framework for viewing individual incubator operations	4.77	5.11	0.34
Response options: 1 = very low degree to 7 = very high degree			

Table 7.4
External Orientation of the Central and Northern Incubator Group

Goal Clarity	First Questionnaire Mean	Second Questionnaire Mean	Difference
The Incubator Group:			
Incubator managers have a clear understanding of CN group goals.	3.85	4.82	0.97
Response options: 1 = strongly disagree to 7 strongly agree			

Table 7.5
Network Orientation of the Central and Northern Incubator Group (continued)

Table 7.5 *(continued)*

Identity	First Question-naire Mean	Second Question-naire Mean	Difference
We've all been part of groups where a feeling of solidarity or "all for one, and one for all" exists. To what extent does this feeling exist from belonging to the CN incubator group?	4.83	5.53	0.70

Response options: 1 = very low degree to 7 = very high degree

Holism

Which statement in the following list most accurately describes relationships among CN group incubators at present?

	First Questionnaire		Second Questionnaire	
	Number	*%*	*Number*	*%*
Individual incubators operate entirely on their own	1	7.7	0	0
Individual incubators operate on their own with a little help from each other	7	53.8	2	16.7
Individual incubators operate on their own with some help from other incubator	5	38.5	8	66.7
Individual incubators operate with quite a bit of help from other incubator	0	0	0	0
Extensive interaction among incubator occurs under the umbrella of the CN group	0	0	2	16.7

Response options: 1 = very low degree to 7 = very high degree

Part IV
Developing a Network of Community Organizations

8

Developing the Inter-Church Network for Social Concerns

This chapter describes the work of a network of church organizations that has developed in a small rural town since early 1993. At that time, a retired minister issued an invitation to representatives from the "social concerns" committees of several churches to meet to discuss social issues and the work taking place to deal with them. I was one of these representatives. Since that first meeting, the Inter-Church Network for Social Concerns (INSC) has gradually developed as an interorganizational system. Representatives have met regularly and have become involved in several collaborative efforts to affect broad positive change in the community. In addition, the network has contributed to progress in a number of areas. I have been an active member of the INSC steering committee since the first meeting and chaired the group in 1995–1996. In these roles, I have helped develop and manage the network, and also have helped design and facilitate several key events and activities.

Creating the Network

A series of critical events triggered and influenced early network development. This section briefly describes these events and their impact on the network.

Recognizing a Problem

Dr. Benz (a fictitious name), a retired minister and seminary professor, identified the need to form an organization among churches to deal with broad social issues facing the community. Dr. Benz had grown up in the town and had strong ties to the community and the seminary located there. His professional work had taken place in various parts of the United States, including California and Kansas, before he returned to town as a professor at the seminary.

After his retirement, Dr. Benz reflected on the status of the community and how to use his beliefs and values as a platform for positive change. During an interview, he stated that he has always had a strong belief in social action through laypersons in the church—a belief that change occurs horizontally through committed ordinary members rather than through hierarchical formal church organizations. His assessment of the existing community situation over several years led him to conclude that the local "Ministerium," the organization of clergy that meets to coordinate joint church activities, had no history or concept of collaborative action to bring about social change. Consequently, Dr. Benz decided to attempt to create a new organization to link the church lay committees that deal with community social issues. First, he went to the Ministerium to gain their understanding of his intention and to obtain access to the social concerns committees in the various churches. Next, he issued an invitation for each committee to select representatives to attend an exploratory meeting on forming some type of organization. The following section gives information on the first meeting and early development of the network.

Convening Organization Representatives

On April 14, 1993, Dr. Benz convened an "Exploratory Meeting of Social Concerns Committees of Some Rural Town Churches to Look at Possible Cooperation." Eight representatives (including me) of four churches, an Episcopal diocese, and two social issues organizations (County Human Relations Council; Interfaith Center for Peace and Justice) attended the exploratory meeting. Representatives discussed several topic areas including preliminary expressions of interest and possible directions for cooperation, ongoing work of the two community social issues organizations, and the existence of common concerns and a willingness to collaborate to address them. Representatives exchanged much information and learned about several potentially relevant community needs and activities. For instance, several participants mentioned racism in the community as a concern. At the end of the meeting, individuals agreed to meet again a month later to continue discussion of the need and desirability of forming an organization to deal with shared concerns.

The second event in building the network was a meeting in May 1993. Despite an attempt to broaden membership by inviting four additional churches to send representatives, again, eight individuals attended. Participants agreed that there was a continuing need to meet, and they formalized the name of the new organization as the Inter-Church Network for Social Concerns. Following up work at the first meeting, considerable discussion of racism again took place. Participants tentatively discussed the possibility of a meeting or conference on this subject. Representatives expressed general support for the idea and assigned joint responsibility for this potential shared activity to the social concerns committees of two member churches. Representatives defined the network role as providing input and support to the effort. This decision helped establish from the outset primary network functions of identifying, focusing attention on, catalyzing, and helping organize activities on community-wide issues that require action of several organizations to address. Providing information exchange among churches on social issue activities emerged as another key function. Adopting these functions rather than assuming the role as a primary direct action organization has been crucial to enabling the network to contribute to dealing with broad community issues.

Developing the Network

The next two meetings in the fall of 1993 gave further shape to the network and its role. Discussion of several topics was particularly important here. To illustrate, the representative of the Interfaith Center for Peace and Justice (ICPI) presented a formal proposal to use that group's newsletter to communicate information about network activities, social action committee work in member churches, and general information on community social issues. In return, INSC member churches would provide direct financial support for the newsletter. After considerable discussion during several meetings, network representatives decided to use the newsletter as one of several ways of relating to the community. However, the network was unwilling to become too closely linked to the ICPI by adopting the newsletter as its own and providing continuing financial support. This decision helped establish the role of the INSC as a bridge among existing organizations, not an integral part of any of them.

Discussion of racism in the community continued at this meeting. Dr. Benz introduced a brief tentative proposal to sponsor a community event that would educate and sensitize participants, help prepare them to take action, and foster communication among town and county leaders on racism and discrimination. Specifically, the statement proposed the following:

> Hold a one-day conference in 1994, inviting all members of cooperating churches with a special effort to include (perhaps as leaders) those who hold responsible positions in the local community. Included in this conference could be such elements as an inspiring address, reports from the County Human Relations Council, and minority representatives on local conditions, small group discussions of issues and personal attitudes, a look at the Christian mandate, a plenary discussion of next steps.

This general proposal sowed the seeds of a major INSC activity covered in detail in the next section. Working on this activity had a major impact in defining and developing the network and its role in the community. It also triggered action on an important local issue.

Starting with the first INSC meeting, representatives also reported on social issue activities taking place in their churches. For example, one person reported on the soup kitchen for homeless people run by her church. Another described work of members with Haitian migrant workers in a local fruit orchard. Other general events (e.g., Summer Peace Camp for children and an annual Heritage Festival) or needs (e.g., prisoners' support after release) also were shared at network meetings. Information sharing provided knowledge of what was happening in the community on key social issues. Discussion also built a shared understanding of issues and a context for considering possible ways of dealing with them. Several of these information-discussion topics have led to later INSC work.

Our Schools: Open and Inclusive?

This section describes the largest project the network has sponsored to date. As indicated above, racism in the community arose as a key issue during the first few INSC meetings, and active work on this issue has continued through various community groups. The following subsections cover network activities to help bring about change in this area.

Design Work

Holding an open meeting for leaders and members of the community to examine the community racial situation was the guiding concept of the first proposal. A second version of the proposal emphasized an historic contribution of the town in establishing and expanding the American vision of equality and challenged local citizens to examine the present situation from this perspective: "How is the historic vision of unity and equality faring today in our community?" Network members discussed the proposal, raised several questions about it, and appointed a small planning group to design and plan the event.

As discussions took place in planning group sessions and regular INSC steering committee meetings, the basic design principle gradually changed. The original process proposed to have leaders from several key local industries (e.g., banking, real estate) talk about their efforts to improve interracial relationships: What initiatives are they taking? What forces impede their efforts? What could the INSC do to help improve their efforts? In short, the design revolved around formal leaders of key organizations. Discussions in several planning group and steering committee meetings revealed serious questions about the proposed design:

- What are the actual experiences of minority group members in the community?
- What perspective will the conference take—minority group or white?
- Will minority group members participate in the conference?

Discussing these questions and other aspects of the proposed conference led to a gradual shift in conference design. Inputs from the minority community had a major impact in causing this change. For example, an informal leader of this community stated that minority members would not attend the conference as originally proposed. Later, she joined the planning group and participated in devising a new conference design.

Based on extensive discussion in the planning group and suggestions/questions from me, the new design emphasized an open search process that would actively involve stakeholders in exploring and defining critical aspects of race relations in the school system. Briefly stated, the revised approach was constituent centered, an approach that seemed desirable because (1) the exact nature of the problem was unclear and (2) the willingness of the community to work on it uncertain. Renaming the meeting a "consultation" instead of "conference" reflected the new design principle.

First Workshop

After several additional planning group meetings, considerable discussion in the steering committee, and inputs from minority community leaders, the basic design of the meeting emerged. Designing, planning, and making arrangements for the workshop took place over a ten-month period. General workshop design required using a facilitator to help coordinate and manage activities, and meeting this need was discussed in several planning group and SC meetings. The group decided to select someone who was not involved with INSC to ensure neutrality. Several group members proposed names of people they knew to serve as facilitator. I suggested Dennis Bellafiore, who, as indicated earlier, has worked as a close colleague on New Baldwin since early 1993. Eventually, after discussing various candidates during several meetings, the group selected Dennis, and he and I played a strong role in designing the first workshop.

A greatly modified search process guided the six-hour Sunday session on October 9, 1994. Selecting individuals to participate in the workshop was a crucial design feature. Several selection criterion were used.

- *Stakeholder representation:* The committee identified teachers, students, parents, the school board, school administrators and staff, and citizens as primary stakeholder groups involved with the issue and selected key individuals from each of these.

- *Minority community representation:* Since the minority population of the town is relatively small, the committee paid special attention to identifying as many potential non-white participants as possible. A minority community leader who was a member of the planning committee gave many useful suggestions here and made many personal contacts to encourage participation.

- *Balance:* Workshop design also called for relatively equal representation from various stakeholder groups to ensure that different points of view were heard. The committee also used gender and distribution among various churches and member organizations as secondary selection criteria.

Invitations and Pre-Work. Approximately 45 individuals received written invitations to the meeting almost three months before the event. As Figure 8.1 indicates, this letter explained the general nature, purpose, and scheduling of the meeting. Network Steering Committee members used phone calls to follow-up the written invitation and talk with potential participants about the meeting. One week before the workshop, participants received a final reminder letter that reconfirmed details of the meeting and stated several general

July 15, 1994

Dear

With this letter, we are inviting you to participate in an important event to be held Sunday, October 9, 1994, 3 pm to 9 pm, at the (Church), (Address).

The Inter-Church Network for Social Concerns, the sponsor of this event, has been concerned about the rising tide of intolerance in our society. It reaches into all sectors of our private and public life. Because of their impact upon the coming generation, our schools are a critical area for addressing this issue. We are, therefore, planning a consultation on the theme, "Our Schools: Open and Inclusive?" We hope you will be among the 30-40 educators, parents, students, minority group representatives and concerned citizens who will be participants.

The format for the consultation is designed to encourage free and open exploration of issues by all who attend. It is our intention that, by the end of our time together, we will have reached a consensus on concrete steps that all of us can take toward making our schools more "open and inclusive." Mr. Dennis Bellafiore, a skilled and experienced group facilitator, will guide us through the process.

Please give the invitation your serious consideration. All expenses, including a light supper, will be underwritten by the churches in the Network. A member of our committee will call you in the near future to obtain your response.

Sincerely,

(signed by members of the planning committee)

Figure 8.1
Invitation to INSC Workshop

areas for discussion. The letter asked participants to reflect on these primary discussion areas before the meeting.

The Workshop. Thirty-one individuals participated in the workshop, with fairly equal representation from various stakeholder groups. Figure 8.2 outlines the workshop design. Workshop activities occurred in the total group and four concurrent heterogeneous small-group sessions.

October 9, 1994
Welcome
Statement of Purpose
Outline Workshop Activities
Describe Discussion Guidelines

Small Group Work

Task 1   Think about the changes that are coming in the economic, political, social, technological, and environmental areas on a local, state, and national level. As you look at the challenges ahead for the Rural Town Community, what do you see as having a large impact on the public school system?

Task 2   Take a few minutes to quietly reflect on the current state of race relations in the Rural Town public school system. What words, images, phrases best characterize the present situation?

Task 3   If you could design the ideal public school system for Rural Town, what would it look like in terms of race relations, interactions, communications and involvement for students, teachers, staff, administrators, board members, parents and community members?

Task 4   What issues need to be addressed to move from the present situation to the ideal school system?

Total Group Work

Task 1   A member of each small group presents a brief summary of outputs of group work emphasizing issues identified to move to an ideal school system.

Task 2   Each small group lists issues identified to move to an ideal system under appropriate constituent categories (student, teacher, parents, administrators, school board members, staff, community members) on flip chart paper posted on walls.

Dinner   Participants self-select into small groups and talk informally during dinner.

Task 3   Participants circulate, read issues posted on flip charts, and vote for the three "most important" issues.

Figure 8.2
INSC Workshop Design
A Consultation—Our Schools: Open and Inclusive? (continued)

Figure 8.2 *(continued)*

Small Group Work

Task 1   What actions on the part of the community must we initiate, continue, or eliminate in order to address the priority issues regarding race relations in the public school system?

Task 2   As you look at the totality of actions required to bring about a change in the race relations in the Public School System, what is required for these actions to come about?

Total Group Work
Small Group Reports
Summary and Next Steps
Closing

Following Dr. Benz's welcome and statement of purpose and Dennis's explanation of the flow of work and meeting ground rules, participants met in the four subgroups. A trained facilitator worked with each group to help stimulate, focus, and support open discussion. I facilitated work in one group and helped manage the workshop. Ideas generated were recorded on flip charts for later work. Having representation of various stakeholders in each small group assured diverse inputs. It also ensured that sharing occurred across stakeholder group boundaries. Discussion guidelines fostered open sharing of views and helped maintain participants' interest and involvement. Following the general phases of the search process, workshop events started with an exploration of environmental factors, examined the current situation, defined an ideal school system, identified issues involved in moving from the present situation to the ideal system, and began to map action steps. Figure 8.2 includes statements and questions used to stimulate participants' responses during each stage of the workshop.

Participants actively engaged in responding to questions and discussing issues. In many cases, time constraints caused facilitators to end sessions before discussion had finished. At the end of the workshop, participants generally made very positive comments about participating in the meeting. Many also expressed a belief that the work could help bring about changes in the school system and indicated a willingness to participate in follow-up meetings.

Outcomes. Responses of workshop participants about the current state of race relations in the school system gave cause for concern. Typical comments showed the following concerns:

- Hypocrisy and racism of silence
- Lack of dialogue between racial groups
- Continued lack of staff (and teacher) diversity
- Low expectations of minority students
- Ignorance-unconscious racism, sexism, etc.
- No celebration of Martin Luther King holiday

Despite the less-than-rosy picture of present race relations in the school system, workshop participants had clear ideas about improving the school system. For example, in an ideal system, students would be blind to color or ethnic group membership, groups would form according to members' interests, and individuals would respect each other. In the teaching area, there would be more minority teachers, and teachers would encourage and accept all students. In addition, teachers would have a global perspective and use books that emphasize diversity. Administrators would establish racial balance in hiring teachers and staff and include black members at the decision-making level. Administrators would also emphasize teaching tolerance as part of the curriculum and establish clear policies against acts of racism. School board members would also use diversity to establish an enriched educational community. Observing Martin Luther King Day as a school holiday received special emphasis. Identifying key aspects of an ideal school system generated much energy among participants, and they indicated a desire to continue work on the issues identified. At the same time, past failures to make progress made some individuals skeptical.

Second Workshop

Following the workshop, written outcomes were content analyzed and typed, with copies sent to all participants. Meanwhile, the planning committee decided to hold a second workshop in early December to follow-up on the key issues identified and develop more detailed action steps for dealing with them. An invitation to participate in this meeting accompanied the copy of notes from the first conference. I chaired planning committee design work and facilitated the workshop.

Sixteen individuals participated in the two-hour second meeting. Stated workshop goals included increasing clarity and understanding of priority issues, agreeing on general action steps for one or two areas, and defining detailed plans for carrying out actions. Discussing how to organize to continue work over time was also on the agenda.

After the introduction process, activity in the total group focused on assessing the current state of work. This process began with a brief review of earlier activities and the top four issues from the October workshop. Attention then turned to identifying important relevant events that had occurred in the community since the first meeting. Among them was a school district retreat to initiate the strategic planning process for the system. Participants noted that discussions during the retreat covered several topics from the October workshop (e.g., diversity is a strength—how do we increase staff and curriculum diversity?).

During the second phase of the workshop, participants self-selected into two small groups to discuss and make plans for dealing with the two top priority issues:

1. How to re-educate, train, and increase the awareness of teachers, staff, administrators, school board members regarding diversity.
2. How to change the curriculum of American history and other courses to include all people.

During small-group discussion, Group 1 selected a strategy of encouraging workshop participants to volunteer as action team members for the school district strategic planning process to begin in January 1995. Specific steps called for participants to sign up for, recruit, and distribute applications before the December 20 deadline. The second issue group recommended forming small groups comprised of students, teachers, and administrators in each school building to monitor the climate of human relations. Several small-group members volunteered to organize this effort.

Third Workshop

At the end of the December meeting, participants decided to meet again in late spring to assess progress on implementing action steps from the previous workshop and to make further plans. The group chose May 21 to allow time for completing the formal phase of the school district strategic planning process. I coordinated planning group design work and facilitated the meeting. Thirteen individuals took part in the two-hour meeting. All work during the session occurred in the total group.

Participants reviewed actions from the strategic planning process that relate to openness and inclusivity in the school system. Several specific accomplishments were noted, especially the action plan described in Figure 8.3. This plan committed the school district

Specific Results:

The District will develop a program for the entire school community in order to cultivate respect for the worth and dignity of every person, and to affirm ethnic and cultural diversity and to combat racism and other forms of discrimination within the school district.

# Action Step (Number each one)	Assigned To	Starting Date	Due Date	Completed Date
1. Appoint a committee representative of the diversity of the community, including administration, staff, parents, and volunteers from the community, to design implement, monitor, and evaluate the action steps which follow.				
2. Plan and provide in-service training for all board members, all staff and all administrators around the topic of "Our Community's Diversity and Uniqueness."				
3. Review, revise or, if necessary, develop policy and guidelines for the district that affirms ethnic and cultural diversity. Principals will submit a yearly report to the assistant superintendent stating compliance to the guidelines.				
4. Procedures to be followed when incidents involving racism or other forms of discrimination in action or speech arise will be developed.				

Figure 8.3
School District Action Plan on Diversity (continued)

Figure 8.3 (*continued*)

	Assigned To	Starting Date	Due Date	Completed Date
5. Present programs to staff and students which promote appreciation of cultural and ethnic diversity and raise awareness of the continuing problem of racism in our society and community. Speakers and resources from the community such as the Dean of Intercultural Affairs at (local) College, and from such agencies as the (County) Human Rights Commission should be utilized. Parents and other community volunteers should be used whenever possible in the planning and presentation of such programs.				
6. Provide a workshop for teachers at all grade levels to assist them in developing thematic units that blend multicultural concerns and ethnicity within the existing curriculum.				
7. Provide training to administrators in recruiting persons from minority groups as student teachers, teachers, administrators, and classified staff.				
8. The committee will coordinate with those responsible for the professional Staff and Classified Staff Induction Plans to be certain that information regrading the ethnic and minority makeup of the community is provided to all new staff.				
9. The committee will evaluate the program every two years and make recommendations for its continuation and modification.				
10. As part of the development and evaluation processes, the committee will contact other school districts for ideas and possible coordination of training and programs to reduce the cost per trainee.				

to develop ways of supporting diversity and respect for the inherent worth of all individuals. Specific action steps to bring this about included in-service training for board members, staff, and administrators, developing procedures for dealing with incidents of racism, and training for recruiting minority group members. Figure 8.3 describes other planned action steps including procedures for following up on, monitoring, and evaluating progress.

Workshop design also asked participants to share their expectations about positive outcomes from strategic planning actions. Perceptions varied considerably with an average of 4.7 on a 1 (nothing will happen) to 10 (all recommendations implemented) Likert scale. Sharing reasons for individual ratings triggered much discussion. Discussion revealed a general feeling of hopefulness tempered by considerable skepticism based on past lack of progress.

For the future, the group agreed to address the school board on key issues, to support a Human Relations Council (HRC) project to increase the number of minority applicants to county schools, and follow-up on work started during the strategic planning process. In addition, the group identified making Martin Luther King Day an official school holiday as a specific goal. Participants considered and rejected the idea of developing a special action-oriented network organization to attempt to reach this goal. Instead, they expressed support for using existing relevant community groups to devise a broad based strategy to make this happen. One INSC member volunteered to contact the County Human Relations Council to explore its interest in adopting the holiday issue change project.

Observing a New School Holiday

This section describes work of the county Human Relations Council to have the local school district adopt Martin Luther King Jr. (MLK) Day as an official school holiday. Strictly speaking, this work goes beyond the role of the INSC. However, it provides an example of successfully transferring action taking responsibility from an interorganizational network system to an existing community organization. The case also demonstrates many basic similarities between conceiving of the network and the HRC project and developing strategy and action steps to affect change. Overlapping membership (three individuals, including me, are members of both the INSC and HRC steering committees) has helped orient thinking and provide follow-through in devising a strategy and action steps consistent with the philosophy and principles used during the three workshops described above.

Word about INSC workshops spread through the community. This information plus a contact from the network liaison caused the county Human Relations Council to call a September 1995 meeting of several individuals to explore interest in devising a strategy and action steps to bring this about. Two other network steering committee members and I participated in this exploratory meeting.

For over ten years, various individuals and groups had tried unsuccessfully several times to influence the school board to adopt MLK Day as an official holiday. One attempt approximately five years earlier almost succeeded with four Board members voting for and five against observing the holiday. These unsuccessful efforts made most HRC steering committee members highly skeptical about the likely success of the current effort. On one hand, they believed the change was important for the community and were committed to it. It also is consistent with their values and beliefs. On the other, they found it hard to believe that success was possible and tended to focus on arguments of community members opposed to the change (e.g., "students should be in school learning about Dr. King on his birthday"). After lengthy discussion at several later meetings, the steering committee adopted making MLK Day an official school holiday as an action project. Figure 8.4 describes some of what happened in reaching this decision. Eventually nine SC members volunteered to work on this project and the group began work in November 1995. Members selected me to chair the group, the "Rubber Meets the Road Group."

Developing a Strategy and Early Action

Figure 8.5 highlights key events in the change process that led to having the school board decide to observe MLK Day as a holiday. Identifying the problem and creating a vision for the future had occurred during the INSC workshops. However, the Human Relations Council group had to decide to become involved and take action to attempt to bring about the change. Individuals had to coalesce as a group around the vision generated in the earlier workshops and make it their own.

Based on early work in the fall, the group began to develop its strategy and preliminary action steps for 1996. Previous work, con-

Having the Human Relations Council (HRC) steering committee decide to accept making Dr. Martin Luther King Jr. Day an official school holiday was far from a straightforward process. Participants in the first meeting in September indicated a strong interest in adopting this as a change project. As an outsider to the HRC, I was energized by this expression of "enthusiastic support" to work on making the day a holiday, and thought that the decision had been made. Later events showed that this wasn't true. [Incidentally, the September HRC steering committee meeting was the first time this group had met in many months.]

The HRC began to call regular steering committee meetings in October and invited me to attend. I agreed, assuming that working actively on the school holiday issue would be the main topic of discussion. Instead, discussion covered a wide variety of topics and failed to focus on any of them. This continued for several meetings, and when the holiday issue came up, individuals either skirted it or gave reasons why the school board would never approve it. Eventually, I ended up being the only strong advocate of working on the issue. Other members had become more interested in becoming a study group in which individuals shared and explored their attitudes and beliefs on racial issues. Several of them brought in published materials on how to organize and run such groups.

I had become extremely frustrated, at this point, and felt that we were getting off the track and letting the community down by not trying to make MLK Day an official holiday. We had an obligation to follow through on it since it had stemmed from the INSC workshops. In my frustration, I blurted out that, while I supported others' interest in a study group, I did not wish to devote time and energy to that activity. Instead, I wanted to make the rubber meet the road by working hard to make the MLK Day holiday a reality. The SC responded by forming two groups: The Study Group and the action or Rubber Meets the Road Group (RMRG). Everyone except me participated in both groups. At the request of the SC, I agreed to chair the RMRG and continued in that role during the change process. It proved to be an extremely challenging role that required much on-the-job learning. The Study Group ceased to function in early 1996.

Figure 8.4
Forming the Rubber Meets the Road Group

- Identify the problem
- Create a vision for the future
- Decide to act
- Organize to take action
- Define change strategy and first action steps
- Test community attitudes and perceptions
  Contact several key community leaders
  Feedback and discuss contacts
- Reaffirm decision to affect change
- Broaden support for change
  Develop outline to guide discussions with community members
  Contact community members by phone or in person
  Feedback and discussion of outcomes
  Identify additional key organizations, groups, and individuals
- Align action steps with school district schedule for developing school calendar
- Make informal contacts with key school board members
- Plan final action steps to influence school board decision
  Write and distribute letter to community members
  Write and stimulate writing articles and letters in local newspapers
  Organize presentations and appearances at school board meetings
  Catalyze and support work of key community groups (e.g., Ministerium, Interfaith Center, high school students)
  Stimulate phone calls and letters to school board members
  Coordinate work with minority community
- Outcome: School board decides to observe MLK Day as an official holiday for the next two academic years
- Future action: Institutionalize school holiday in the community

Figure 8.5
Key Events in Change Process: Making MLK Day an Official School Holiday

tacts with community leaders, and discussion led to adopting a strategy of appealing to the higher community values of fostering diversity and respect for individual and ethnic differences. This emphasis built upon the philosophy statement included in the school district action plan contained in Figure 8.3:

> The District will develop a program for the entire school community in order to cultivate respect for the worth and dignity of every person, and to affirm ethnic and cultural diversity, and to combat racism and other forms of discrimination within the school district.

As indicated earlier, an INSC member chaired the school district strategic planning action team that developed this statement in the spring of 1995.

Another aspect of the strategy involved identifying key community groups and leaders within each who were likely to support the holiday idea. The basic approach was to surface, demonstrate, and build support through contacting likely sympathizers in key constituent groups. Persons contacted were asked to influence other individuals and the organizations and groups to which they belonged. Beyond teachers, administrators, and other direct constituent groups of the school district, the groups identified included the Chamber of Commerce, selected members of the college faculty, editor of the local paper, local service group leaders, lawyers, and various community opinion leaders. Work placed special emphasis on identifying and involving key members of the minority community through continuous communication with informal leaders.

To start taking action, group members contacted a few leaders in community organizations to test support on the holiday issue, identify attitudes/perceptions, and enlist their help. These contacts provided much encouragement. For example, discussion with the new principal of the high school suggested strong support for the holiday. And, the local Ministerium expressed support for the holiday and offered to send a representative and write a letter to express this view to the school board. General reactions from community leaders led the group to reaffirm its decision and redouble its effort.

Broadening Support

The next action phase involved broadening community support for change. First, a list of approximately 30 individuals in key organizations and groups was developed. Later, contact work led to expanding the list of over 50 key individuals. A request by several group members led to developing an outline to guide individual conversations with community leaders. The outline included the background of the effort, strategy being used, current status, asking for personal and organizational support, and recruitment of others for the change effort. Developing and having the discussion outline helped members gain understanding of the process of contacting community leaders and helped reassure them of their ability to conduct the discussions.

Group members reported the quality and outcomes of contacts at biweekly meetings; discussing these contacts provided ongoing learning and triggered new ideas for further action. Virtually every person contacted expressed support for making MLK Day a school holiday and most of them volunteered to help. This buoyed group members' confidence greatly and motivated them for additional work.

Final Action Steps

After determining approximately when various decisions on adopting the school calendars for the next two years would occur, the HRC group began to plan final steps to influence the school board. A first step involved several informal contacts with school board members. Beginning in September, the HRC group began an intensive community campaign to affect change. Important parts of this effort included the following:

- Organizing presentations by individuals from various groups at each school board meeting between mid-September and November 4, 1996. The number of presentations varied from 5 to 12 per meeting. The HRC group also organized supporters' attendance at each of these meetings. The size of these groups of supporters ranged from 10 to approximately 40.
- Contacting newspapers to ensure coverage of school board deliberations and action on MLK Day. At first, the town paper provided little coverage of the issue. Later, after several contacts from our group, this paper provided extensive coverage.
- Writing and stimulating writing of articles and letters to the editor in two local newspapers.

- Triggering and supporting work of key community groups to influence the school board. For example, following a request from the HRC group, 11 members of the Ministerium wrote a letter to the school board expressing support for the MLK holiday. Later, a local newspaper published the letter on the editorial page after an HRC group member contacted the paper and urged publication. In addition, two high school students set up a card table in the cafeteria and discussed the holiday proposal with other students during lunch periods. In addition, they took the initiative and designed and conducted a student survey of 426 juniors and seniors that showed overwhelming support (approximately 80 percent) for the holiday. They also organized eight student presentations, including results of the student survey at the November 4 school board meeting.

- Sending letters to several hundred key community members requesting them to write and phone school board members, attend Board meetings, write letters to the editors in local newspapers, and urge colleagues and friends to give active support to the change effort.

A groundswell of support resulted from these and other actions, and approximately 40 pro-holiday supporters attended school board meeting on November 4, 1996. Still, several amendments to the holiday motion were made and many arguments given against it at this meeting. After all this, the final result of this two-year effort was having the school board vote 5-4 to adopt Dr. Martin Luther King Jr. Day as an official school holiday for the next two academic years. Work to institutionalize the holiday began in early '97.

Other Network Activities

Working to explore and help bring about change in the public school system represents the largest effort by the INSC so far. At the same time, the network has played a key role in several other important community efforts.

Community Soup Kitchen

One member church had operated a soup kitchen to provide free lunches to homeless and needy persons since late 1991. Church volunteers provided the staff that prepared and served food and cleaned up after lunch. A representative of the sponsoring church described

soup kitchen work and issued a call for volunteers and food donations from other churches at the first network meeting. Updates on
soup kitchen activity occurred at later meetings. Other INSC representatives took information back to their churches and as awareness
grew, over time, volunteers and food donations from member
churches increased. Members of various churches signed up for specific days of the month and provided volunteers to prepare, serve,
and clean up on those days. Gradually, as involvement of members
from other member churches increased, the soup kitchen began to
become viewed increasingly as the community soup kitchen, rather
than as that of a specific church.

A key event in development of the kitchen took place in 1994.
Due to an increasing number of clients and limited space, the sponsoring church triggered a community-wide evaluation of the needs
and organization of the soup kitchen. All network member churches
involved in the project participated in this review and evaluation
process. After considerable discussion over several months, participating churches established the Community Soup Kitchen with a
multichurch board of advisors and a paid part-time manager. The associate pastor of a member church served as the first board president.
This new organization has solidified member church involvement
and increased general awareness of the soup kitchen and the need for
it in the community. In effect, the kitchen has become institutionalized in the town as a valuable community resource.

The INSC played a key role in transforming the Soup
Kitchen. Existence of this group provided an effective way of identifying the need for multichurch action, communicating about the
need, and organizing among churches to meet the need. It also provided support from a total community perspective for individual
church involvement.

Prison Project

In April 1994, an INSC member voiced a "desperate need" for a volunteer support group to work with inmates of the county jail. Her
idea involved forming a group to support prisoners during the transition back into society. Network SC members discussed various aspects of the prison situation and the proposal and agreed to continue
to examine and discuss the issue. Two months later, members decided to study the feasibility of adopting prison ministry as an INSC
project. Several individuals offered to work on an informal committee to carry out this task.

Members of the committee met with the prison warden during the summer. This discussion at the prison identified several needs and concerns of ex-prisoners. Stated needs included help in finding jobs and housing, literacy training, and obtaining support from Alcoholics Anonymous.

By October, the committee had gathered material on a well-established prison ministry program in another county of the state. In addition, the committee had identified and contacted an existing group, the County Prison Ministry Task Force, that was working on other aspects of the prisoner situation. To avoid duplication of effort, the Task Force shared information on their work and offered to collaborate in helping the network plan its next steps.

Two outside individuals involved with prison ministry work participated in the January 1995 network SC meeting. The associate director of the State Prison Society gave a brief history of the organization and summarized its purpose and current programs. He also described what resources and support the society could provide to local groups interested in organizing services to prisoners and their families. A member of the County Prison Task Force also attended the meeting. Both outside representatives stressed the need for services for prisoners, particularly immediately before and after release, and the importance of local community awareness, involvement, and support. Members of the INSC prison committee agreed to continue to explore effective ways for member churches to respond to inmate needs.

Based upon earlier work, the prison committee reached a tentative decision to establish a local chapter of the State Prison Society. Discussion among network members indicated that different churches were at various stages of readiness to act on this decision. Hence, the committee sent information and a request for volunteers to member churches. This action was designed to educate, test interest, and allow motivated individuals and groups to start work. Ten persons expressed interest in serving as volunteer visitors to inmates after receiving training from the State Prison Society. Educating church members about prisoners' needs and recruiting additional volunteers continued.

The County Prison Society became an official organization in September 1995, with a network representative as co-convener. Local society members met with the warden and indicated their intention to follow-up on all prisoner complaints (a primary function of local prison society organizations). By July 1996, ten local prison society members had received training and been issued official visitors' cards. Local society activities expanded beyond prisoner visits to include working with women prisoners to provide support for making craft items and decorating children's clothing for distribution through "Wee Care" to needy children, revising the handbook for prisoners, and collecting paperback books from various organizations for the prison library. A local store displays and sells inmates' craft work with individual producers receiving 75% of the selling price. Society work planned for the future includes providing writing instruction to prisoners and cosponsoring an art contest with the County Arts Council.

In brief, the Local Prison Society has become an established functioning organization in a relatively short period. The network played an important role in bringing to the surface the need for working with prisoners, in helping communicate and educate church members about the need, and in facilitating and supporting establishing the local prison society chapter. It continues to provide ongoing support and a ready means of communicating with member churches about prison society work and prisoner needs.

Refugee Resettlement

Late in 1994 network representatives undertook the task of resettling several refugee families through member churches as a community social action project. As Figure 8.6 indicates, this decision followed from several prior events. During the previous ten years, three member churches, acting independently, had sponsored Vietnamese families and helped them resettle in town. Several network members mentioned these experiences during an early meeting as examples of individual church social action work.

Identifying the Problem. By mid-1994, media reports had caused many individuals to become aware of the situation in the former Yugoslavia and the fact that there were a large number of Bosnian refugees. This awareness highlighted a probable need and prompted discussion during a steering committee meeting of possible network action. Consequently, representatives returned to their churches and presented the idea of having each church sponsor a refugee family. Receptivity was mixed: One church was enthusiastic about the prospect, another was interested but doubtful of their ability to be successful due to size, and two others were lukewarm. Other member churches did not express interest. The

1988–1992	Three member churches independently sponsor refugee families.
1993	Network representatives mention sponsoring refugee families as examples of earlier social action.
Mid-1994	INSC representatives discuss idea of providing support for sponsoring refugee families as a community project.
Mid–late 1994	Representatives return to member churches, present and discuss refugee proposal, and test for support.
Late-1994	INSC adopts supporting refugee resettlement as community project.
March 1995	One member church commits to sponsoring a refugee family, three others express interest.
April 1995	Network arranges meeting of interested churches with a regional church social agency professional experienced in refugee resettlement.
Apr–May 1995	Representatives share detailed information on and discuss resettlement with church committees.
May 1995	Network decides to support sponsoring refugee families from Vietnam.
May 1995	Second member church commits to sponsor refugee family.
August 1995	Social action committee of third church meets with regional church social agency refugee resettlement professional.
Sept 1995	Third member church commits to sponsor refugee family.
Oct–Dec 1995	Vietnamese Refugee families arrive in October, November, and December.

Figure 8.6
Sequence of Events in the INSC Refugee Resettlement Project (continued)

Figure 8.6 *(continued)*

Oct 1995– June 1996	Member church committees provide direct assistance to refugee families (housing, finding jobs, education, language instruction, health care, etc.). INSC provides system for exchanging information, sharing experiences, developing solutions to problems, and linking individual refugee families.
Jan 1996	Network sponsors community buffet covered-dish dinner for the three new refugee families.
Ongoing	Sponsoring churches maintain contact with refugee families and assist them in dealing with major problems (e.g., locating permanent housing, moving). Members discuss status of refugee families during INSC meetings.
Oct 1996	One member church sponsors a second Vietnamese refugee family.

network SC interpreted these reactions as encouraging and adopted supporting refugee resettlement as a social action project for the following year.

Educating Member Churches and Developing Commitment. Early the next year, the first member church made a definite decision to sponsor a refugee family. A network representative from this church also arranged for a professional resettlement staff member of a regional religious social service organization to meet with interested INSC members. At the meeting, the resettlement professional gave details about a sponsor's role, functions, tasks, and responsibilities, and distributed several information sheets that described them. This person also answered questions and described the support her regional organization would provide to back up sponsors. This meeting led participants to have a much clearer understanding of the resettlement process and the responsibilities assumed by a sponsoring church. Defining a target of helping refugee families become basically self-sufficient after three months of direct support was particularly useful. Awareness of this target helped dispel fears of assuming a never-ending obligation. INSC representatives used the detailed information about sponsorship and reassurance from the meeting to conduct further discussions in the social concerns committees of their churches.

Discussion also caused network representatives to reconsider an earlier tentative decision to sponsor Bosnian refugees. The resettlement professional pointed out that the strongest need existed for sponsors of Vietnamese families. She also indicated that 1995 marked the last year for Vietnamese to immigrate to the United States under a special State Department program. Member church representatives brought this new information back for discussion at the next network meeting. The additional information plus the fact that several Vietnamese families had settled in the community several years earlier led to the decision to sponsor resettling families from Vietnam. Presumably, the established families could help bridge the communication gap between sponsors and the new refugees, who were likely to speak little or no English, and also provide social support. As events unfolded, help from Vietnamese already in the community was invaluable in getting the new families resettled.

Taking Action. By September, three churches had decided to sponsor refugee families and organized for their arrivals in October, early November, and December. Each church had arranged for temporary housing, provided warm clothing and a small basic food supply, and made plans for medical care, social benefits signups, locating jobs, transportation, interpreters, and many other aspects of daily living. By the end of three months, two of the three families were essentially self-sufficient.

In January 1996, the network sponsored and coordinated a dinner for the three families, other Vietnamese from the immediate and surrounding communities, and church members involved in resettlement. Approximately seventy persons, including about thirty Vietnamese, attended the event. All Vietnamese families brought special foods to the covered-dish dinner and took great delight in introducing us Americans to these new dishes. Observation and comments indicated that the dinner was a joyous event for organizers, sponsors, and guests.

Network Role. What was the INSC role in the resettlement effort? What did the network contribute that individual churches could not have done on their own? While it is impossible to answer these questions definitively, the network appears to have made a difference in several areas.

- Participating in the network informed several representatives and member churches about previous refugee sponsorship. Several persons, including me, were unaware of this happening. Later, when the potential need to resettle refugees arose, members related the need to previous experience that showed "it could be done."

- Adopting resettlement as an INSC project helped develop support among Network representatives ("We're doing this together and learning in the process"). Over time, discussing sponsorship in meetings increased understanding and reduced anxiety of representatives, who then were better prepared and more confident in proposing that their individual churches support a refugee family. The fact that other churches would be doing it also helped allay church members' fears and provided a model for action ("If they can do it, so can (should) we!"). In brief, the network helped create a new social reality regarding the desirability of sponsoring refugees and the possibility of successfully resettling them in the community.

- The network provided a system for communicating, sharing, and learning about resettling refugee families on an ongoing basis. This made individual church efforts easier by not having to reinvent solutions to the same problems.

- By supporting the refugee effort, INSC helped sensitize the community to the needs of people around the globe. The Vietnamese refugees were persona non grata in their home country due to their involvement with the United States during the war. Reaching out by helping them resettle in the community had a very positive impact on those directly involved. For example, over 40 people volunteered to help resettle the family adopted by one member church and they learned a great deal through providing assistance. Many of them seemed to gain at least as much from the experience as the refugee families. Increasing the number of Vietnamese members also has enhanced ethnic diversity in the total community.

Outcomes of INSC Work

Since its beginning in April 1993, the INSC has achieved several goals:

- Convene and establish the network as a functioning organization.
- Become recognized in the community as a positive force for change.
- Bring a community-wide perspective to key issues/problems.
- Sponsor, design, convene, and manage three workshops to assess and deal with existing race relations in the public school system.
- Transfer (successfully) primary responsibility for action on the Dr. Martin Luther King Jr. holiday project to the Human Relations Council.
- Support and participate actively in developing and carrying out the Human Relations Council change effort that caused the school board to adopt Martin Luther King Day as an official school holiday.
- Increase community awareness and support of the soup kitchen, and help convert it to the Community Soup Kitchen supported by over twenty local churches.
- Raise the level of awareness of representatives and member churches to the need for activities with county prison inmates.
- Help establish and support a local chapter of the State Prison Society to serve county prison inmate needs.
- Reveal a need, trigger action, and provide general support to an effort of resettling three Vietnamese families in the community.
- Serve as a system that provides a forum for continuous dialogue on broad social concerns among member church representatives.
- Help develop and maintain a community-wide sense of responsibility and perspective for dealing with important social concerns.
- Provide leadership, expertise and human resources for dealing with key community issues.

Conclusions

It is possible to reach several conclusions based upon INSC activities and experience in working as a system member since its inception. This section describes these conclusions briefly.

1. The INSC was convened to help member churches collaborate to improve the community through social action. At the outset, this group was conceived of not as a network system but rather as a more traditional type of organization. Over time, though, the system has taken on the essential features of an interorganizational network. For example, in dealing with key issues identified, the network has surfaced and defined the situation and devised ways of bringing together the stakeholders required to deal with them. So, the emergent role of the system has become to identify, define, and develop consensus about broad-based community issues, help focus attention on them, and provide support by helping design effective ways of dealing with them. The network provides a way to help churches, other community organizations, and the community-at-large deal with broad social issues. Experience with the INSC indicates that such a network organization can play an important role in stimulating and leveraging the actions of other "doer" organizations in a small, relatively conservative rural town.

2. Experience with the INSC suggests that devoting time and attention to developing a network as a system is desirable but it may not be absolutely essential. Ideally, devoting time and attention to system development work should be an integral part of building and maintaining the network. However, for various reasons, this is not always possible. Initially, conveners of the INSC conceived of it as a traditional action-taking organization. By facing broad community issues, discussing them, and grappling with ways of dealing with them, other possibilities became apparent. Working to design and conduct the three workshops on public school openness and inclusivity was particularly important. Starting from a traditional design, gradually, the design process became based on the socio-ecological network model and followed basic steps of a search process. This came about through design work in the planning

group, discussion in steering committee meetings, broadening the planning group to include a minority community leader, direct participation in workshops, and follow-up work on the outcomes of the workshops. In short, work to develop the network was done primarily through the process of engaging in the work of the system. The network has conducted almost no work directly on development per se.

3. Members have experienced working on network activities as highly motivating and involving. A relatively small number of individuals participate in INSC work on a regular basis. Seven or eight representatives from seven member churches and two community social action organizations typically attend SC meetings, for example. The INSC appears to provide them with meaningful ways of tackling broad-based issues beyond those that exist in individual churches and community organizations. Network capacity to provide meaningful involvement also extends to participants in specific events such as workshops and the soup kitchen. Experience suggests that many persons in the community desire to make a difference by helping to devise and implement positive steps for change. The INSC offers ways for them to participate in making a difference.

Part V
Learnings and Implications

9

Learnings from Working to Develop Network Organizations

The previous eight chapters covered work done to develop three network organizations for different purposes in varied settings: (1) the New Baldwin Corridor Coalition, which involved developing an interorganizational network to bring about economic and social change that creates and sustains a twenty-first century manufacturing community; (2) the CN group, a time-bounded process designed to create a network organization among 14 widely dispersed, independent local business incubators; and (3) the Inter-Church Network for Social Concerns, a way of organizing to bring about community change.

In this chapter I will reflect on my experiences in working with these three distinct development efforts. I will attempt to highlight learnings that cut through the three situations.

Learning 1: Using Network Concepts Is Crucial to the Development Process

Figure 1.1 identified key features of the socio-ecological view of interorganizational networks. These network concepts provided a powerful framework for thinking about and taking action in the three situations covered. For example, orienting work to the problem domain level—a level above that of interorganizational relationships—was crucial in all three situations. In the New Baldwin case, this level of thinking is required to match the level and complexity of change—creating a twenty-first century community. In addition, this perspective fits with the vision-based approach of development work. Using the vision of an ideal community has stimulated the development process and helped motivate many people to become involved in the effort.

Directing development of the CN group to the total network level was required to get local incubator managers to break their frame of thinking about relating to only one or a few other incubator managers and begin to conceive of higher level regional and statewide issues. Such thinking also was required for the Inter-Church Network for Social Concerns to start identifying and working on community level issues and to design interventions to deal with them. To summarize, using a model that focused development work at the appropriate level was critical in all three cases.

Other features of the socio-ecological approach also enabled development in these situations. Loose coupling allowed members to participate and explore new ways of working together without a threat to the identity and autonomy of their home organizations. Having members responsible for all network activities including developing a shared understanding of the organizational purpose and large-scale problems/issues as well as planning and managing work also greatly reduced fears about working together. Since membership is voluntary and each organization is free to join or leave as it chooses, little risk from network membership exists. At the same time, the potential for positive experiences that can result from working with others to bring about high level change toward member-defined goals is virtually limitless. Thus loose coupling contributed to developing all three of the networks.

Treating network organizations primarily as conceptual systems or referent organizations was also generally important. Adopting a referent organization stance is consistent with the defined New Baldwin mission, values, and operating principles. Essentially, New Baldwin exists to help foster collaboration among existing organizations that causes change toward a new community. Hence, having a basis for new ways of thinking and operating is crucial. The socio-ecological approach has provided this conceptual foundation. In the CN group case, the socio-ecological view was used from the beginning to develop the action research proposal and plan and build the network. Building on this perspective, network development work emphasized the importance of members having new ways of perceiving and experiencing their local organizations within the larger network system. Developing new ways of thinking was a prerequisite for beginning to act differently among themselves and toward the outside world. Over time, the CN group began to function as a combination referent and action-taking group.

At the outset, the basic nature of the Inter-Church Network for Social Concerns was unstated. Reverend Benz saw that community churches were not sufficiently engaged in working on large-scale social issues and convened representatives to address the situation. Initially, representatives viewed the network as a primary action group. Only through working on issues and projects has the role of the network as primarily a referent organization crystallized. This stance has strengthened the organization and enabled it to help the community address several broad social issues more effectively than before network existence.

Briefly discussing application of three key features of the socio-ecological perspective of networks merely illustrates the contribution of this approach to developing these systems. Other features also played an important role in the development of the three networks. For example, serving as a forum and having the capacity to convene and provide professional resources to help design and facilitate major events was important in all three situations. Unfortunately, space limitations do not allow discussing application of additional features in detail. However, it is clear that having an appropriate conceptual framework is crucial to intervening effectively to affect change. And, the socio-ecological view of network organizations is a useful guide for conceptualizing, planning, taking action, and learning from addressing complex issues beyond the organization level.

Learning 2: Network Members and Outsiders Often Experience Difficulty Understanding Networks

While using socio-ecological network concepts was essential to guide development work in all three cases, the approach also caused difficulties. One of these stems from the largely conceptual nature of these systems. In the early stages, members frequently ask "What is this organization?" and "What are we supposed to do?" Questioning the nature and role of the network was a recurring issue during the first two years of New Baldwin. Only during the third and fourth years of work did steering committee members begin to understand and get comfortable with the network role. Even today, questions about the nature and role of New Baldwin arise from time to time.

At the start, CN group members questioned the need for a network organization ("We're already doing it"), identified the potential network with existing groups (e.g., the Pennsylvania Incubator

Association), and asked repeatedly about its purpose and function. Only through engaging in the process of developing the network, exploring possibilities, and inventing its functions and activities did members come to understand and accept its role. In essence, the CN group became what members made it.

At various times, Inter-Church Network members have raised similar questions about role, functions, and activities. Questioning was most prevalent during the first year and a half. However, discussions of specific situations and working on various issues and projects have caused members to understand the primary network role: identifying, focusing attention on, catalyzing, and helping organize activities on community-wide issues that require action of many organizations to address.

Ingrained images of organizations and organizational work also caused difficulties. As Karl Weick (1979) noted, Americans seem to absorb bureaucratic concepts about organizations at a very early age. In addition, since many members and stakeholders work in organizations with traditional bureaucratic design features (e.g., hierarchy, defined jurisdictions), networks do not "feel right" to them. The horizontal member-controlled design is one cause of difficulty. In the early stages, members experience stress from not having clear understanding of who's in charge. Later, members begin to recognize that "We are the network, and we're in charge," which creates a different form of stress that results from feeling responsible but not knowing quite what to do (role ambiguity).

Stress also arises from the often indirect, intangible nature of work. Individuals inside and outside networks tend to think of work as making tangible things happen. This action bias can lead to an "activity trap"—busily engaging in activities that give the illusion of accomplishment but are not appropriate for the network. For instance, in the early stages of New Baldwin, many groups and task forces were active in trying to make things happen. This activity may have been necessary for members to work through and discover the emerging network role. At the same time, lack of an internalized network vision and mission, a rough model of key network features, and processes for examining and reexamining the organization could have led to considerable activity that added little value to the community.

Paradoxically, the features of network organizations that make it possible for them to contribute to resolving complex high-level issues also make it difficult for members and outsiders to understand these systems. There are several ways for network organizations to deal with this phenomenon:

1. Clearly identifying the interorganizational network model guiding the development process
2. Orienting new members to key features of the model
3. Conducting early interventions that encourage exploring and identifying an appropriate network role and activities
4. Conducting additional interventions to reexamine, discuss, and reinforce general understanding of the network role and activities at critical points in the development process
5. Devising effective ways of communicating the nature of the network, its role and activities to stakeholders and other key organizations, groups, and individuals in the community
6. Monitoring and evaluating network activities versus the adopted network vision and mission and making necessary changes continuously

While the socio-ecological view provides a general framework for thinking about and developing an interorganizational network, it does not prescribe what to do in particular situations. The nature of each network is unique and emerges from development work and task activities over time. Still, understanding the basic nature of the type of system being built is crucial.

Learning 3: Using Action Research Is Essential

Descriptions of the three network organizations emphasized the importance of using an action research approach. Experience in developing the New Baldwin Coalition, CN group, and Inter-Church Network confirms this observation. Designing and conducting AR on a continuous basis is required to develop and maintain networks over time. Working to develop the three networks covered reveals several important features of action research.

AR as an Orientation Toward Network Development. Rather than being a distinct activity, action research is a perspective or orientation for engaging in network development. Ideally, the approach pervades every network member, group, and activity. It also should become an integral part of the thinking and behavior of network members. Action research for network development is an ongoing process of planning, taking action, questioning, reflecting, searching, and creating and capturing learnings. Questioning, reflecting, and building learnings into the network can occur during any phase or part of the total action research process. Using action research to create and maintain networks as learning systems emphasizes a process of proactive engagement, not simply reactive adjustment.

Action Research as Planned Processes. Action research required to support network development involves devising periodic processes that generate information about specific activities or overall system functioning. Several such processes were important in the three cases covered in this book. For example, using survey feedback to CN group managers was an early step in helping members understand their perceptions of existing relationships among local incubators. In addition, repeating the survey feedback process toward the end of active work with the group provided information on changes in perceptions and attitudes, and on outcomes of the development process. It also contributed to members' learning about the network and its development. Similarly, information from the early survey of business managers helped guide New Baldwin development. In short, AR for network development involves formal clearly identifiable processes—periodic data generation, feedback, discussion, planning, action taking, data generation processes—and far more.

Action Research and Opportunism. Developing interorganizational networks requires identification of situations that may offer possibilities for increasing understanding. Some situations present obvious opportunities for enhancing understand and learning. The three Inter-Church Network workshops on school district openness and inclusivity illustrate this type of event. Others, such as how the New Baldwin Corridor Coalition should respond to an external threat, require (1) inventing ways of getting members to see things in different ways and (2) creating action steps that reflect and reinforce the new insights. In this situation, it was important to preserve the concept of making a decision that would advance the interests of the entire community, and avoid taking action that increased conflict among various organizations (i.e., to maintain an ecological perspective rather than regressing to an interorganizational view). Developing such an integrative solution took considerable insight, creativity, and effort by New Baldwin leaders and others.

　　Spontaneous Network Development Indicators. Often, important indicators of network development occur spontaneously. For example, a member's statement about the presentation to the state board of the primary funding agency, "This is the first time we really had to pull together to do something for all of us," captured CN group feeling of having reached a new level of development. Such naturally occurring happenings may reveal more about the development of a network than carefully designed action research interventions such as survey feedback. Similar spontaneous events indicated new stages of development or learning in the other two cases. In short, individuals involved in developing networks must remain alert for various kinds of information about the state of the system and identify it for possible learning by other network members.

　　In conclusion, experience indicates that using an action research approach is absolutely essential to foster continuous network development. It is virtually impossible to conceive of building and maintaining a network and having the system carry out activities over time without AR. The types of action research required to support developing interorganizational networks fall toward the open, complex, and difficult to manage ends of conceptual dimensions that Max Elden and I devised to analyze several earlier diverse AR applications (Chisholm and Elden, 1993). Hence, effective AR processes must constantly be invented and discovered. Using action research as an integral part of the network development process is extremely challenging.

Learning 4: Effective Design Work Is Essential

Developing network organizations requires devoting constant attention to designing events and activities. The importance of designing major development events effectively is fairly clear. At the same time, the design of ordinary events and activities is also crucial since they educate members and outsiders and help define the future nature and course of the network.

　　Designing Major Events. Several major events illustrate how design work may be used to advance network development. The strategic planning meeting, the review and assessment of 1994 work, the interactive community meeting, and several other meetings represent key events in the development of the New Baldwin Corridor Coalition. The three development conferences were important events designed for the CN group, and the three workshops on school district openness and inclusivity served a similar purpose for the Inter-Church Network for Social Concerns. In each case, a small design team comprised of various network members and OD professionals developed the basic designs for the events. Key design dimensions included:

- Determining the strategic purpose of the event: How does the event build upon previous work and advance network development?
- Defining goals: What should the event achieve?
- Identifying participants: What organizations are essential to deal with the issue? Who should represent each stakeholder?
- Determining location: What location is appropriate for the event? What climate will the facility help create? Will the physical features fit with activities of the event (sufficient space, breakout rooms, etc.)? Is the location convenient for participants to reach?
- Selecting the convenor: Who should convene the meeting? Who symbolizes concern for the whole system? Who is viewed as a legitimate convenor?
- Determining internal design features: What are the critical features that will affect outcomes of the event?
  Structure of meeting
  Process-flow and sequencing of activities
  Required professional resources—facilitators, experts, etc.
  Guidelines for the meeting
  Written materials and audiovisual equipment required
- Selecting and inventing specific development interventions: What specific techniques fit with overall design features?
- Defining time dimensions: When should the event be held and how much time should it take? What time constraints do participants have?

Design team discussions of these and other design-relevant topics that inevitably arise require considerable time and work.

Designing Routine Events for Learning and Development.
Developing network organizations also requires effective design of
normal events and meetings. For example, Dennis Bellafiore and I
usually prepare a tentative design for regular New Baldwin steering
committee meetings. Typically, Ike Gittlen and one or more other SC
members participate in this premeeting design work, which involves
reviewing happenings at the previous meetings, assessing the status
of task accomplishment and network development, and devising possible ways of advancing task accomplishment and coalition development. Premeeting work focuses on designing questions, identifying
topics, planning the sequencing of activities, and other interventions
that encourage members to learn or consider things from a new perspective.

Chapters 6 and 7 described several instances of designing normal events to develop the CN group as a network organization. One
example involved designing the steering committee meeting several
weeks after the first development conference. Part of the meeting requested members to reflect on the CN group and identify learnings
from development work conducted to that point. This process helped
crystallize and share existing learning, it created new insights about
the network and its development, and it helped establish a norm of
questioning, reflecting, and learning from happenings in the system.
We used this approach whenever possible during the CN network development process. These two applications merely illustrate ways of
designing ordinary events to advance the development process. Over
time such design work has important cumulative effects on developing networks by modeling ways of learning from day-to-day work
and supporting emergence of norms that support the learning
process.

Design Requires Extensive Interaction. Effective design
work requires extensive interactions among network members and
professional OD personnel. Using a heterogeneous design team for
interventions helps build in and encourage desired interaction. And,
having the design team stimulate suggestions of other network members, steering committee, and external stakeholder representatives
can greatly expand interactions. This extensive interaction among individuals with diverse perspectives enriches designs of development
interventions. Improved designs result from (1) creating designs that
capture more of the complexity and uniqueness of the emerging network and (2) ensuring that members are building their own system.

Learning 5: Developers Must Be Flexible

As indicated above, experience shows the importance of thoughtfully designing major interventions and ordinary events to advance network development. Good design work is powerful. At the same time, individuals working with these systems must be prepared to modify or abandon planned designs based on new information that emerges while working with the system.

Many incidents of this type occurred in working with the three networks. For example, as a last minute "enhancement," Dennis and I developed a process for talking with community participants during the New Baldwin interactive town meeting. This involved giving project leaders at each idea center a short list of questions to ask individuals from the community. After giving a brief description of the project, leaders were encouraged to pose several simple questions (e.g., What led you to come tonight? What's important to you about creating a quality community for the twenty-first century?). The idea was to increase community members' understanding of the coalition, find out their interests and concerns, stimulate their interest in its work, and get them actively involved in New Baldwin work. At the meeting, it quickly became obvious that this design would not work and, as a result, project leaders refused to use it. Instead, they ended up carrying on casual conversation with participants and discussing the projects informally. In retrospect, these spontaneous informal discussions turned out to be a better way of engaging participants than the planned process.

Another incident occurred at the end of the third INSC workshop. The design team proposed setting up a network organization to follow through and take action on items identified during the workshops, and the team proposed a process for establishing this new action-oriented network. However, participants refused to become part of such an action network. This decision had the potential of ending productive work to improve racial relations in the public school system. However, continued questioning and discussion revealed that participants did want to follow through on recommendations from the workshops but felt that creating a new organization was unnecessary. They indicated that an existing organization could catalyze and manage the effort. Hence, one participant agreed to ask the Human Relations Council to lead this effort. As indicated, the HRC eventually assumed the action-taking role and actively engaged in planning, initiating, and coordinating work that led the school board to make

Martin Luther King Day an official school holiday. Again, flexibility in adjusting thinking and the design for future action was needed to continue progress toward the general network goal. Success in this case also required transferring action-taking responsibility to another existing organization.

Learning 6: Integrate Development Work with Normal Network Activities

Previous discussions emphasized the importance of designing AR processes into normal network activities. The same principle applies to system development work in general. Since network members are loosely linked and participate in network activities only sporadically, they are usually reluctant to take additional time for development work per se such as, team building for the steering committee. Of course, this reluctance to participate in straight development work does not eliminate the need for it. So, those responsible for network development must do two things: (1) In the short run, devise ways of tightly integrating it with "real" work, and (2) over the long run, design ways of heightening member awareness of the importance of this work.

One way of integrating development work with normal activities is to use small groups to design and plan events. This approach has been used extensively in all three cases presented in this book. For example, a small design team comprised of me and several coalition members developed the proposed design of the 1993 Strategic Planning Conference. As indicated, I provided information about the nature of search conferences and other development concepts. Through discussions over time, design team members gained an understanding of the search process and began to appreciate the importance of specific work on developing and maintaining the network. Based on internal discussions, the team came up with a proposed design for the conference and discussed it in detail with the steering committee. Several rounds of developing design team proposals, SC discussion of the proposals, inputs from outside individuals, and redesign occurred before the final design emerged. This extensive work contributed to SC and design team members learning a great deal about New Baldwin as a network organization and about ways of working with community participants. Direct involvement in design and planning work also induced learning and understanding of the nature and importance of development work.

Building development work into normal activities also has taken place in the other two cases. To illustrate, a small planning team worked to develop the design for the first INSC workshop on public school openness and inclusivity. Planning team discussions, combined with network steering committee reviews and discussions over a ten-month period, led to the final workshop design. Consistent with the New Baldwin experience, direct involvement in devising a design for the workshop advanced development of the network and contributed to increased understanding of the system and its work. With little or no direct development work, members have learned a great deal about the organization as a network. Members now talk knowledgeably about the network role in identifying broad community issues, raising awareness of them, and creating ways of triggering various combinations of existing organizations to address them. They also have learned to say "no" to requests for involvement in work inappropriate for the INSC.

In summary, experience suggests that in many network development situations, opportunities for outright development work may be limited. Among the present cases, only in the CN group situation was development a legitimized, fully funded activity. Consequently, system development professionals and managers involved in helping develop and maintain networks often must create ways of incorporating development work with other normal organizational activities. Following traditional organization development principles, such a "boot leg" approach is far from ideal. And, it frequently causes me to feel uneasy—Is it overly manipulative to devise an activity aimed at developing a network without having fairly complete understanding and explicit consent of participants? However, experience suggests that in many cases, it is the only way to initiate and carry out network development work. Hence, rather than condemning it, perhaps we must learn to create more effective ways for members to learn about developing the network in the process of starting and carrying out its work.

Learning 7: Building and Maintaining Grassroots Support Is Crucial

Establishing strong ties to the community is essential to developing interorganizational networks such as the New Baldwin Corridor Coalition. The broad purpose for network existence and activities comes from the community-at-large, and the general community provides the resources and support required for the coalition to survive and grow. Fortunately, Ike Gittlen and other leaders who started NBCC recognized this fact and began building broad-based support before convening the first network meeting. Several newspaper articles and news conferences provided information about the problem situation and started educating community members about the need for interorganizational collaboration. This early work also did several other things: (1) it tested the coalition concept among key stakeholder groups; (2) it refined the idea by getting new inputs and suggestions; and (3) it built support of key stakeholders by involving them in building the network. Identified stakeholders included business organizations, labor unions, local, state and federal government, educational institutions, economic development agencies, and community groups.

I heard about the idea of "mining the community" on a National Public Radio broadcast in 1992. The concept connotes much about desirable relationships between a network organization and its surrounding environment. According to this metaphor, mining means three different things:

1. Mining as in digging for physical elements (e.g., coal, iron ore): Tap the resources of the community by involving individuals, groups, and organizations in network activities and generating financial and social support for the work.
2. Mining as in an exploding military mine: Explode ideas and new ways of seeing things throughout the community, have one idea combine with others to create chain reactions similar to nuclear explosions.
3. Mining as in making "mine": Help the network and community develop based on its unique history, traditions, and capabilities, and incorporate the preferences and desires of community and stakeholder members about the future into the development process.

All three aspects are necessary to develop and maintain effective network relationships with the external environment.

Since the external environment is dynamic, maintaining and adjusting relationships with stakeholders over time also is essential to network effectiveness. In the case of New Baldwin, new stakeholders have emerged (e.g., a key community organization), new legislation and government programs have been created (e.g., state legislation on reclaiming "brown field" sites), a new political party has gained control of the executive and legislative branches of state government, and network leaders have discovered new relationships with organizations and individuals that will strengthen the network. The CN group discovered new stakeholders as network members expanded their thinking and analysis of the environment during the development process. Consequently, a network organization must develop ways to evaluate existing relationships with the larger community and invent effective linkages to relevant stakeholders. The New Baldwin strategic communication survey illustrates one way of assessing linkages between a network and its stakeholders. Periodic strategic planning by network members offers another process for reviewing network-community relationships. Those of us involved in developing interorganizational networks must constantly be alert to discovering or inventing other ways of making these assessments.

Learning 8: Developing Networks Requires Creating Appropriate Forms of Organization

Devising a form of organization that is consistent with features of interorganizational networks and reflects the unique requirements for tackling specific large-scale issues in particular settings is extremely difficult and requires considerable ingenuity. While each situation is different, insights derived from the three cases provide general guidance for organizing.

Network Orientation. Network design and structure have major impacts on relationships with stakeholders and the general community. Figure 9.1 illustrates the organization of the New Baldwin Corridor Coalition. At first glance, the chart seems to be disordered and haphazard, but on closer reading several things stand out.

First, the community and various member organizations serve as the hub of the network and its activities. This orientation emphasizes the special importance of the external environment for interorganizational networks. Networks come into existence to deal with large-scale issues that cannot be dealt with via existing organizations or mere interorganizational cooperation. Consequently, as indicated earlier, the total community serves as the foundation and focal point of New Baldwin as a network organization. Recognizing this fact in the organization structure helps orient and maintain members' thinking to the dependence of the network on the total community. Following through by designing and managing activities and events

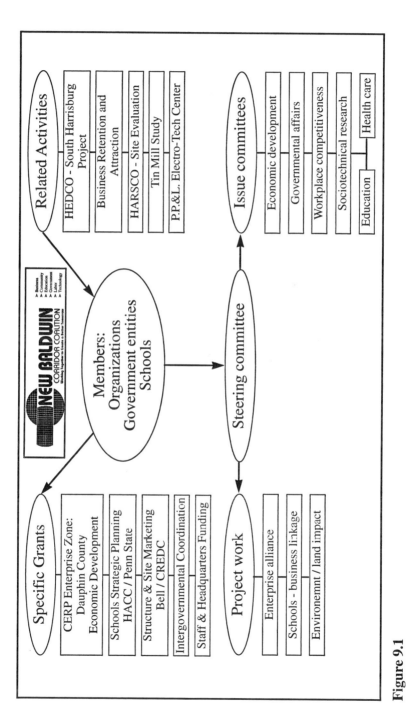

Figure 9.1
Organization Chart for the New Baldwin Corridor Coalition

to involve the community and reflect its needs is also required to make such an orientation a reality.

Steering Committee. A steering committee provides a way to manage overall network activities and guide network development. Representatives of various stakeholders normally comprise the steering committee, which manages overall network activities and is responsible for maintaining and developing projects. Since stakeholder representatives make up the steering committee, this group integrates linkages with key constituents, maintains contact with the external environment, and manages the network as a total system. Experience suggests the importance of being open and somewhat flexible about steering committee membership. For example, the CN group expanded steering committee membership over time as the three local incubator managers recognized the importance of having broader stakeholder involvement and gained trust in the development team and the development process. Similarly, membership on the INSC steering committee has changed as network activities have evolved and the members recognized the importance of including representatives of new groups. In general, it seems desirable to maintain a strong bias toward being relatively open and inclusive versus closed and exclusive. This stance means, "When in doubt, include." Then, let the individuals/organizations involved decide whether or not to continue being involved.

Task Forces/Committees. Forming task forces and committees provides a flexible way of organizing new issues and activities. For example, the INSC set up a small task force to explore prisoner needs and possible network involvement in meeting these needs. This group investigated the situation, reported back to the steering committee and discussed information gathered several times, identified and worked collaboratively with another prison task force, and finally recommended organizing a local chapter of the state prison society. Since forming the local chapter, the network has kept contact with and provided general support to the organization. The network also continues to serve as a means of communicating between the local prison society and member churches.

The education committee of New Baldwin provides an example of establishing a group to explore needs and organize work in an identified area. The original New Baldwin mission statement identified education as an area critical to developing a quality twenty-first-century community. Hence, the steering committee established the education committee in 1992 to bring local districts together to explore needs and determine possible ways of improving the overall quality of public education in the corridor. Based upon the success of its work and the continuing motivation of members, the education committee has become an effective mininetwork within New Baldwin. As indicated earlier, the committee identifies strongly with the coalition and incorporates its vision, principles, and ways of operating. It continues to initiate new activities, such as a proposal to upgrade the computers available in member school districts, and it has jointly sponsored new summer school programs each year. This committee represents a case of successfully disseminating New Baldwin by developing a mininetwork organization in its own image. Developing the Enterprise Alliance is another example of the concept of building a similar network for action in a particular area.

Setting up teams of incubator managers who worked together on defined tasks between CN group development conferences is another case of organizing to reinforce network design principles. The underlying concept was to have members work in the teams as a way of gaining understanding of the advantages of collaborating to deal with network issues and to build trust among team members. Experiences in the teams reflected many experiences similar to those in the total network. Briefly stated, it is important for network developers to foster organizational forms that demonstrate and reinforce key features and principles of networks. These mininetworks help both members and outsiders learn the nature of networks. Broadened and deepened understanding of using these systems to engage higher level issues results.

Coordination. Having a focal point for communication and coordination is also crucial for networks to function, and this coordination (not direction) function becomes increasingly important as a network such as New Baldwin grows and becomes more complex over time. Coordination involves sending out SC meeting notices and distributing meeting notes, handling routine requests for information, managing preparation and distribution of newsletters and special information pieces, and serving as a contact for members and community members. This coordinator is a key staff role required to maintain network communication and helps identify issues that require steering committee attention.

At the start of the coalition, the administrative assistant of a member nonprofit organization served as coordinator in addition to her regular work. For the past three years, a professional staff member of a local university institute has worked half-time as coordinator. A state department has provided funding through a small grant for the work. In short, providing adequate coordination is essential for a relatively complex network organization such as New Baldwin to function.

Coalition experience also indicates the importance of carrying out coordination as informally as possible. Establishing a permanent office with an "executive director" and staff is inconsistent with the mission and nature of the network. Therefore the steering committee decided to use a "bare bones" approach to coordination that relies on substantial support from member organizations. This support includes the local university providing space and equipment and making available professional coordination services. This approach ensures that required coordination takes place without building up a permanent office that requires relatively large funding and constant chasing of grants.

Learning 9: The Process of Developing Networks Is Disorderly and Nonlinear

Writing on OD and network development tends to depict the process of developing these complex systems as rational, planned efforts that use well-thought out sequences of steps to bring about change. And for the most part this book is no exception. Emphasizing the planned intentional aspects of development is useful because it helps make happenings in real-life cases understandable. At the same time, such emphasis detracts from understanding by making events seem simpler and more subject to direct influence than they actually are. Accounts of several key events earlier in the book attempted to enhance the reality of the descriptions of development work (e.g., NBCC steering committee decision to use a search process for the strategic planning meeting).

Working on developing the three networks covered in the book has impressed on me that the process is not neat and tidy. Rather, it is often disorderly, informal, circular, and serendipitous. Here are some examples:

- *Disorderly:* My belief that the Human Relations Council steering committee had decided to work on making Martin

Luther King Day a school holiday as a change project at the first meeting was based on simplistic straight-line thinking. Positive expressions of support by the five persons who attended the first meeting did not translate directly into acceptance by the HRC steering committee at later meetings. Now it is easy for me to see why. Different makeup of the two groups, lack of involvement of several SC members in the three INSC workshops on race relations in the schools, and some "fear of failure" by several veterans of previous attempts to make MLK Day a school holiday made direct carryover from the first meeting impossible. Hence, HRC steering committee members had to discuss, question, and make the proposed action project their own before signing on.

- *Informal:* Although work in steering committees, design teams, committees, and other official groups was essential in developing the three networks, unofficial informal discussions also have been important. Work on New Baldwin often requires that I phone Ike and other SC members often to check reality or to move action forward. Similar contacts were needed with SC members during the CN group project and with the INSC. For instance, off-the-record discussions with several school board members were essential to map strategy and action steps to get adoption of the MLK holiday.

- *Circular:* As experienced OD professionals know, key issues do not appear at one moment in time and then disappear. Rather, they come up and, left unaddressed or insufficiently worked, return later on. This occurred at the beginning of the INSC when several general issues (e.g., prison ministry, race relations) were identified. These returned later for testing, clarification, focusing, planning, and further work as action projects. Several recurring themes have also arisen, been abandoned temporarily, and then returned later for more work in developing New Baldwin. These include "who are we and what's our role?" and "how should we be organized?"

- *Serendipitous:* To begin with, becoming involved in all three network development efforts resulted from serendipity—involvement came from being at the right place at the right time or stumbling on an opportunity. I did not have a goal or plan to become involved. In addition, several fortuitous things happened to help advance progress in each case. For example, Thoralf Qvale's trip to the United States to attend the Academy of Management meeting in 1992 and his willingness to adjust his plans and meet with Ike and me to discuss New Baldwin led to a major development intervention (the 1993 Strategic Planning Conference).

To summarize, Karl Weick wrote several years ago (1989) about the tendency for organizational researchers to use mechanistic approaches with little appreciation of the often intuitive, blind, wasteful, serendipitous, creative quality of the research process. The same statements apply to network development. Experience suggests that straightforward thinking and direct application of principles are insufficient. Instead, those who help develop networks must be creative by including the intuitive, blind, "nonrational" aspects of the process to devise effective ways of building these complex systems. Remaining open to information from many sources and having extensive informal interaction with various groups are essential to foster these aspects.

Learning 10: It Takes a System to Change a System

I first encountered this insight many years ago in a graduate course on systems theory, and it has helped guide my work with organizations ever since. However, its special meaning for developing network organizations has come from experiences described in this book.

One aspect of this insight has been covered above by pointing out the importance of using design teams to plan key development interventions. Design teams were created to prepare for several INSC and NBCC interventions. The CN group steering committee played this design role in the process of developing the incubator network. Another earlier point emphasized the importance of extensive interaction within and among various groups to create effective interventions. The same is true to sustain a network over time.

Discussion so far has not covered another key aspect of this learning: the need for action researchers to build a base of professional support to help them understand and deal with complexities of helping interorganizational networks develop. This support base can come from several sources:

- *Internal:* Conducting the CN group incubator development project required that, as the research team, Gregg, Tam, and I become a cohesive group. This was necessary for several reasons:

    To provide a forum for openly discussing various possibilities as we helped design and carry out the development process

    To ensure that we assumed and maintained a suitable approach to the development process

    To enable us to maintain a network focus when outsiders attempted to deflect our attention to unproductive work

In short, having the research team as a base of support was needed to provide adequate stability and integrity to the network development process, while remaining open to new developments and ideas.

Neither New Baldwin nor the INSC provided the natural support group that the CN group project did. In contrast, these two projects have involved discovering and creating professional support wherever possible. For New Baldwin, this has occurred in several ways. One has been Dennis Bellafiore's involvement in network development since April 1993. Dennis and I work collaboratively on design, facilitation, and other development work for the coalition, and for the past two years Tam has worked with us as a very able research assistant. We attempt to help New Baldwin develop by participating and observing specific events and overall functioning of the network system. In-depth discussions, arguments, and explanations based on these participant observations enable us to give informed suggestions to the steering committee about future development needs—not that we're always right or are always listened to. But working as a supportive team enables us to share perceptions, check them out with other network members as needed, debate strategy and action step options, and develop suggestions for SC action. Having such a forum and working as a team enables us to perform more effectively than operating alone.

- *External:* A part of Chapter 3 described Thoralf Qvale's discussions with Ike and me about New Baldwin in August 1992. This is one early event that illustrates the importance of Norwegian colleagues who help me stay grounded in concepts about interorganizational networks and the process of developing them. Support occurs in several ways: phone conversations, E-mail, and written material; professional visits and seminar presentations by me at the Work Research Institute in Oslo and by Thoralf, Bjorn Gustavsen, and Henrik Finsrud at Penn State Harrisburg; and formal events (e.g., symposia presentations) and informal discussions during an annual preconference workshop at the Academy of Management meeting. Ongoing contacts with other professional colleagues help in the same ways.

To summarize, helping interorganizational networks develop calls for using teams, not working as "lone wolves." Forming teams to design specific interventions is one illustration of this principle. Having a steering committee to formulate plans and guide the overall network development process (e.g., New Baldwin and the CN group) provides a second illustration. In addition, action research/OD professionals need to create ways of maintaining their role and supporting their special perspectives and activities. Both internal and external groups and individuals can help here.

Conclusions

Chapter 9 describes several general learnings derived from work to help develop the New Baldwin Corridor Coalition, the CN group, and the Inter-Church Network for Social Concerns. The key examples include the following:

1. Using network concepts is crucial to the development process.
2. Network members and outsiders often have difficulty understanding networks.
3. Using action research is essential to developing network organizations.
4. Effective design work is essential to the network development process.
5. Developers must be prepared to revise designs based on emerging conditions.
6. Much development work must be integrated with conducting normal network activities.
7. Building and maintaining grassroots support is crucial to network development.

8. Maintaining and developing networks requires creating appropriate forms of organization.
9. The process of developing network organizations is disorderly and nonlinear.
10. It takes a system to change a system.

Interorganizational networks are extremely complex systems that are constantly evolving from internal forces (such as learnings from past experience and key decisions) and pressures and changes in the external environment. The openness and loosely linked nature of networks increases the dynamism of these systems. Consequently, there are few, if any, permanent solutions to the organizational issues networks face. Learnings from previous direct experiences and from those of other networks provide starting points for working out appropriate action in specific new situations and under changed conditions.

10

Toward the Future: Networks to Deal with Emerging Issues

The growth of knowledge is a key feature of the postindustrial era, and the need exists for organizations to develop knowledge through proactive learning processes and supportive cultures to match the complex, dynamic environments faced. Appropriately developed interorganizational networks offer an effective way of generating learning that leads to knowledge creation. Resulting learning and knowledge creation can take place at the individual, organizational, and network levels.

Globalization represents another leading feature of the new age. Many signs of globalization are evident in the economic sphere. Rosabeth Moss Kanter (1995) notes that, increasingly, individual firms operating within regional interorganizational networks must invent ways of developing intangible assets (e.g., concepts, competence, and connections) that enable them to compete in international markets. Beyond economic activity, an increasing number of problems are emerging as global issues. According to Cooperrider and Bilimoria (1993), an issue is "global" because (1) its effects extend well beyond national boundaries (e.g., spread of the HIV virus), (2) responding effectively to the situation requires mobilizing human and physical resources from various countries (e.g., severe floods in India), or (3) both. The presence of rapid communications systems heightens awareness of local or national problems around the world. Awareness may in turn lead individuals in various countries to become concerned and start work to deal with identified problems. Networks offer one potentially effective form of organization for working on many global issues.

This chapter covers two recent network development projects involving broad issues that have special relevance for the future. The

214

first is the Nordvest Forum that began as an attempt of employers in a remote region of Norway to deal with a shortage of qualified managers. Nordvest Forum has developed into a broadly based learning network that fosters international competitiveness of the region. Information on the Nordvest Forum comes from Hanssen-Bauer and Snow (1996). The second case covers the Collaborative Alliance for Romanian Orphans. This interorganizational network developed to deal with a crisis situation following the collapse of the Romanian government in 1989. Analysis of the Romanian orphans program provides insights into how developing a network organization can help deal with key global issues. Details about developing the Romanian orphans program appear in Bilimoria, Wilmot, and Cooperrider (1996).

Each case provides insights that can contribute to our growing knowledge about developing interorganizational networks. These examples also provide encouragement to invent, discover, and develop forms of networks to deal with the increasingly complex, broad issues emerging in the late twentieth century.

Nordvest Forum

Nordvest Forum (NVF) was set up as an interorganizational network in 1989. The network includes many of the relatively small to mid-sized companies located in a region on the northwestern coast of Norway. Alesund, a small city, serves as the economic center of the region. Leading industries include fish processing, ship building and marine equipment, and furniture manufacturing. Its coastal location and industrial mix have made the region highly dependent on international trade. Dependence on foreign markets makes the region especially sensitive to organizational changes required by international competition.

Organization

The stated purpose of Nordvest Forum is "to improve regional competitiveness by upgrading the management capacity of the shareholding companies and other firms in the region" (Hanssen-Bauer and Snow, 1996, p. 417). This mission statement reveals several important features of the network:

- *Purpose:* NVF has the broad goal of increasing competitiveness of the region as a whole, not just that of individual member companies. Organizations are loosely linked to the network and can join or leave it at will.

- *Membership:* Both member and nonmember companies are included in the scope of work. This reflects the broad regional network orientation shown in Figure 10.1.
- *Strategy:* The network consciously adopted a strategy of triggering and supporting learning to improve the professional capabilities of managers in the region. In short, NVF defined itself as a broadly based learning network.

Planning and developing the network and its activities began in 1989 and continued during 1990. Nordvest Forum, Inc., established in 1989 to manage network activities, defined its role as a facilitator of learning and change. A full-time managing director and two part-time senior management training and development professionals have carried out much of the basic design, facilitation, and coordination work of the network. To supplement these professional resources, NVF members made an early decision to use resources of member organizations and other appropriate institutions heavily. This decision was consistent with the primary facilitation role: using the network to identify required resources and provide strategic guidance rather than building up a large central staff of service providers. Consequently, a relatively large number of professionals and institutions have provided needed expertise or services to the network over time. Using professional resources from many different organizations and institutions has built and strengthened relationships within the network. It has also stimulated developing linkages to important outside sources of help. Both of these have enriched what Coleman (1990) defines as the social capital of the region.

Programs and External Relationships

Two programs have served as focal points for network activity during the early years of NVF. The Management of Change Program, which began in 1990–1991, requires each participant to engage directly in an organization development project. Projects typically involve having a manager attempt to facilitate change in some key aspect of the organization that will increase the company's capacity to compete internationally. For example, a manager might work on improving interdepartmental relationships or relationships with key suppliers. An experienced manager from a participant's own firm or another network company serves as a mentor on each development project. This requirement reinforces the network concept of using multiple perspectives and resources to deal with local internal problems.

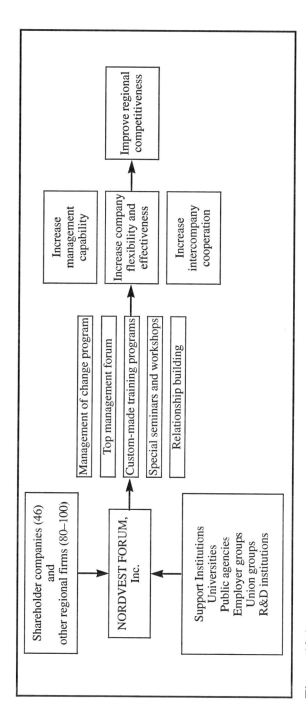

Figure 10.1
Nordvest Forum: Components, Activities, Objectives, and Purpose

Source: Hanssen-Bauer and Snow, 1996, p. 417. Reprinted with permission of Organization Science.

217

The second program, the Top Management Forum provides time, space, and designed activities that allow senior executives to discuss regional issues, learn about international management topics, and develop personal and professional relationships. The two-day Top Management Form meetings occur periodically. NVF also aids organizations in the region in developing special training programs and sponsors special seminars and workshops. In addition, the NVF pays special attention to building relationships required to develop the network and participating firms as learning organizations.

Developing strong relationships with outside resource and support organizations and institutions has been another key feature of the network. For example, NVF has built the capability of bringing in leading experts on organizations and management from many parts of the world. NVF has also emphasized establishing and maintaining linkages with research institutions in Norway, Europe, and the United States. For example, as Figure 10.1 shows, from its inception, the network has developed and sustained support from leading Norwegian business, union, and research institutions. Working with employer, union, and research organizations to hire two University of Trondheim doctoral students in management in 1992 illustrates this commitment to broad collaboration. These students work with member companies on an "as needed" basis to increase understanding of new organization/management concepts and to facilitate organization development. After several years of successful experience, the forum arranged support from the Norwegian Research Council for three more doctoral students. This decision indicates the success of using an organization development approach through joint applied-academic action research in NVF organizations. Using doctoral students to assist network organizations also improves students' professional education and skills and adds to the knowledge base of the region and country.

Outcomes

Evaluation work by Hanssen-Bauer and Snow (1996) identifies outcomes of NVF. Several measures indicate the relative effectiveness of the Nordvest Forum in increasing regional competitiveness through enhanced management capabilities. Surveys of member organization managers and their mentors show that positive outcomes of network activities took place at three levels:

1. *Individual:* helping managers form professional interpersonal networks

2. *Organizational:* fostering change through organization development
3. *Regional:* improving general perceptions of the region in the business press

Other positive outcomes of NVF work include the following:

Developing projects supported by funds from a central employer federation or by business development grants from the Norwegian government. Government or business chose several of these projects as showcase examples of successful business development.

Over ten member companies have used network resources to carry out strategic change of their organizations.

Clusters of organizations have formed mininetworks to foster exchanging information, learning, and working out solutions to common problems. This phenomenon has occurred spontaneously.

Recently, the National Research Council decided to fund action research to support, facilitate, and capture learnings from the future development of NVF.

The network has developed the capacity to influence key resource and policy institutions in the external environment.

These and other outcomes indicate some of the success of the network as a learning and change system.

The Collaborative Alliance for Romanian Orphans

This section covers work conducted to organize multiorganization efforts to intervene in a crisis situation that surfaced in Romania in 1990. The policies of dictator Nicolae Ceausescu's 24-year rule had led to a collapse of the Romanian health care system. Part of the situation involved over 140,000 infants and small children who were virtually left to die in state run institutions. A national policy of demanding that women bear at least four children, combined with a deteriorating economy led to the crisis. Conditions led to abandonment of thousands of children. Many of them had at least minor physical and mental abnormalities. The government created an "orphanage" system to respond to the flood of abandoned children. However, these "orphanages" generally provided inhumane treatment. To illustrate, the budget allocated the equivalent of 30 cents per year for each child's health care. The October 5, 1990, edition of the ABC TV program "20/20" focused attention on the situation. The program reported that at a "Home for the Deficient and Unsalvageable" over 40 percent of the children died during their first year in the institution. "The children were shown spending their days in crowded rooms. Many were dying from lack of medical attention; others developmentally delayed by the sheer lack of human touch. Ten percent were said to test HIV-positive" (Bilimoria, Wilmot, and Cooperrider, 1996, p. 11).

Early Response

World Vision, based in the United States, is a private voluntary organization that has operated in Romania since 1977. At that time it had established relief operations in the country to deal with devastation from a severe earthquake in Bucharest. Operating primarily through local churches, World Vision helped give medical assistance, repair buildings, and train citizens to provide these services. Immediately after the "20/20" TV program, donations of money and goods and offers from volunteers flooded World Vision. These donations enabled the organization to begin immediate relief work, which included sending food, clothing, blankets, and medicine valued at over $8 million.

The size and complexity of the relief effort also caused organizational problems. First, success in having scores of separate relief organizations respond quickly to the crisis overloaded Romanian political, economic, and social agencies that approved establishing operations in the country. Second, certain well-intended obvious "solutions" (e.g., adopting orphans) turned out to cause more problems than they solved. Third, experiences during the early relief work led to recognizing the need for strategic action through basic improvement of the health care system. A special need for educating and training health care workers was identified. In short, early engagement of the problem situation caused a change in emphasis from direct assistance to support for developing Romanian capacity to handle the problems.

Strategic Development

Recognizing the need for strategic intervention through developing the health system led to building a knowledge alliance, the Integrative Program Development (IPD). This organization developed a large network of formal and informal alliances of diverse organizations from various sectors and countries around the world.

IPD's purpose is to develop a self-sustaining system among different organizations scattered around the globe to deal with local issues. These organizations have come together around a shared vision of providing for the total developmental needs of Romanian children.

Thinking and action planning used a four-phase model to guide the transition from emergency relief to a knowledge alliance. Figure 10.2 identifies the four phases (emergency relief, rehabilitation, community empowerment, and knowledge alliance) and gives key system features present during each phase. For example, through the phases, primary situational concerns progress from relieving immediate suffering, to rebuilding indigenous systems, to reversing despair and social disintegration, to developing shared understandings of global issues. Similarly, time frames lengthen from immediate for emergency relief to indefinite for knowledge alliances. Different stages of development also require distinct orientations to guide management thinking and action—from logistics management, to transferring technical knowledge/information, to group and community development, to a network or alliance of a wide variety of organizations. Organizational role also changes during the transitions from the doer role of relief work to the bridging role of the knowledge alliance. In general, forms of required organization change from relatively simple traditional systems for emergency relief to nontraditional network forms for knowledge alliances.

Developing IPD as a knowledge network required constructing vision and mission statements to build linkages with various organizations throughout the world. Two primary programs resulted from this work.

- ROSES (Romanian Orphans Social and Educational Redevelopment Project) has provided direct services to children and paraprofessional and professional training to those responsible for delivering services to institutionalized children. Consistent with the IPD strategy, ROSES placed heavy emphasis on developing the capacity of Romanian agencies and institutions to provide required services.
- MERP (Medical Education Redevelopment Project) has replenished the Romanian medical information system, which government policy had isolated from the rest of the world since 1974. Under this policy, medical journals, books, and information from the West were banned during the 1974–1990 period.

	(I) Emergency Relief	(II) Rehabilitation	(III) Community Empowerment	(IV) Knowledge Alliance
Situational concern	Immediate suffering	Breakdown of indigenous system	Despair and social disintegration	Shared global problem/opportunity
Time frame	Immediate (weeks/months)	Moderate (1–2 years)	Long-term (2–3 years)	Indefinite (beyond program life)
Chief actors	PVO	PVO plus contract professionals	PVO plus local community	All synergistic knowledge sectors
Management orientation	Logistics management	Technical transfer	People-centered "group development"	Multiorganizational alliance across sectors
Core knowledge mode	Compassionate knowledge	Professional "migratory knowledge"	Cultural-context "embedded knowledge"	Integrated knowledge
PVO role	Doer	Expert-coordinator	Facilitator-choreographer	Bridge: Multiorganizational/multisectional
Organizational boundaries	Clear-stable (unitary)	Clear-stable	Open-reactive	Open-creating (hybrid)
	Development as relatively more "routine work"/unitary organization		Development as nonroutine "knowledge work"/hybrid organization	

Figure 10.2
Foundations of a New Strategic Orientation: The Knowledge Alliance
Source: Bilimoria, Wilmot, and Cooperrider, 1996, p. 209. Reprinted with permission of JAI Press Inc.

Work during the summer of 1990 resulted in an alliance of many U.S. organizations to become part of the IPD effort in Romania. The wide variety of organizations included corporations, various departments from several universities (e.g., medicine, psychology, management, social work), government agencies, nonprofit organizations, and professional associations. A consortium of three organizations funded by USAID managed development work, financial resources, and personnel. In total, over 125 different organizations became involved in the effort.

Outcomes of the Romanian Orphans Project
Several outcomes resulted from work of the Collaborative Alliance for Romanian Orphans:

- *Providing immediate emergency assistance:* Becoming aware of the orphans' plight resulted in a large spontaneous outpouring of various forms of aid (e.g. medical and food supplies). Estimated value of this immediate assistance exceeded $8 million.
- *Developing the ROSES Program:* During the first year, this program trained 250 medical students and academicians and 60 orphanage staff persons. This training improved the care of an estimated 40,000 children.
- *Developing the MERP Program:* In a short period, the libraries of the eight Romanian medical schools became current with the latest research and knowledge by providing advanced CD-ROM and video technologies. These information systems made the last 50 years of information available to medical workers.
- *Building a global network:* Establishing a network of over 125 diverse organizations from many parts of the world and devising a three-organization consortium to coordinate and manage it represent major accomplishments. Work of this global network generated approximately $25 million of direct assistance, supplies, and professional services to help improve conditions of Romanian children. According to Bilimoria et al., "after one year of concerted alliance formation, the neglectful deaths and suffering of Romania's orphans reportedly had ceased." (1996, p. 14).
- *Forming many mininetworks:* Over time, many interorganizational networks began to emerge spontaneously to (1) deal with the complexity inherent in coordinating and de-

livering services, and (2) reflect particular stakeholders' strengths and values. At first, IPD performed the crucial role of convening and supporting these mininetworks. However, as these systems matured, they became increasingly self-managing.

- *Recognizing other applications of networks:* Organization development work in the Romanian orphan situation led to recognizing the potential of using interorganizational networks to engage other complex higher-level problems. For example, this insight led to proposing, successfully, that World Vision support using a network-building approach to deal with the multifaceted problems of U.S. inner cities. Accepting a new frame for understanding and acting was necessary for World Vision to endorse using the collaborative network building approach in new settings: Knowledge, including how to develop and manage interorganizational networks, is a critical component of effectively delivering goods and services.

Conclusions

A review of these two cases leads to several conclusions about interorganizational networks:

- It is possible to develop networks that make progress in dealing with issues at the regional and global levels. Being able to develop systems that help manage activities at these high levels is extremely important in an era of increased connectedness and turbulence. Work in other settings that extends beyond the organization level support this conclusion.

- These cases demonstrate that network organizations provide great flexibility for developing ways to grapple effectively with complex issues that involve multiple stakeholders. One advantage, illustrated by the Nordvest Forum, is in defining the regional domain to include all organizations—both members and nonmembers. Such a broad definition of membership encourages thinking about issues at the total system (e.g., regional) level. It also tends to broaden support in two ways: (1) nonmembers know that the network organization takes a comprehensive view of situations. Hence, their views receive at least general consideration; and (2) since membership is voluntary, non-members can join whenever they wish. Networks also provide great flexibility in assembling the resources required to deal with complex higher-level issues and problems. For example, Nordvest Forum adopted a policy of using outside professionals extensively. This policy helped keep the permanent network organization "lean" and helped keep available knowledge current. Using outside professionals, in turn further developed relationships among network organizations and between the network and external resource providers.

- Mininetworks sprung up in both situations. In Nordvest Forum, for instance, informal clusters of organizations formed around common problems or opportunities to share information or lessons. Both external and internal pressures led to the emergence of mininetworks within the Romanian orphans alliance. The complexity of coordinating work among over 125 organizations stakeholder organizations provided a strong external force for differentiation, and the defined missions and values of individual stakeholder organizations gave further pressure in this direction.

    Two aspects of this process in the two cases are striking: (1) the ease and spontaneity of the process; and (2) the preservation of an orientation and commitment to the vision and purpose of the larger network. These two experiences suggest that consciously developed interorganization networks have the capacity to mobilize substantial resources around a shared vision in ways that preserve sufficient identity of constituent organizations. Again, network organizations demonstrated considerable capacity to respond in unified, yet flexible, and differentiated ways to broad, complex situations that involved higher level problems.

- A key feature of both networks was the central role of learning and knowledge. From the outset, the Nordvest Forum was conceived of and developed as a learning network to increase the capability of individual firms and the region as a whole to compete internationally. Creating and applying knowledge through learning have been viewed as enhancing flexibility and adaptability, thus giving a competitive advantage. In contrast, initial response to the Romanian orphan crisis took the form of providing emergency relief services. This response was consistent with World Vision's traditional way of viewing and responding to emergencies. Fortunately, difficulties experienced during the early response period caused learning that led to reconceptualizing the problem and building Integrative Program Development as a knowledge alliance. A distinctly different change and development strategy resulted from this new orientation. Experience in both cases indicates the power of networks that identify learning, knowledge creation and sharing as central to conceptualizing, planning, and taking action.

11

Concluding Thoughts

Interorganizational networks are an increasingly important type of organization in the late 1990s. This type of system is growing in importance to meet emerging conditions in the environments of organizations. General conditions that foster increased use of interorganizational networks include the complexity of issues and problems, increasing interdependence among organizations and institutions, and an accelerating pace of change. These conditions often create "messes"—sets of interconnected problems that single organizations find it impossible to deal with alone. The complexity of these problems typically defies simple solutions by individual organizations. Forming and developing interorganizational networks represents a way of dealing with these complex problems and issues that require collaborative work by various organizations.

Several factors apply pressures to create interorganizational networks—from technology, growth in knowledge, and globalization, to changing beliefs and values. Existing and emerging information processing and communications technologies make possible the dispersal of organizational units around the world. In addition, transportation and manufacturing technologies will add further pressures toward "placelessness"—the capacity to make virtually everything available anywhere in the world in very short time spans regardless of physical location. Growth in the importance of knowledge increases pressure to invent new work organizations that use and create knowledge, and joining other organizations to form networks can advance this quest. For example, the Nordvest Forum in Norway illustrates an interorganizational network specifically developed as a learning system that increases knowledge in a large remote geographic region.

Realignment of economic institutions to international and subnational levels and the declining importance of nations per se also will encourage developing new organizational forms. The interorganizational network is well suited to meet these new demands of globalization in many situations. Similarly, networks have the capacity of enabling individuals, groups, and organizations to develop and put into practice a new set of postindustrial beliefs and values—beliefs that emphasize interconnection, holism, pluralism, and cooperation. These beliefs are highly congruent with the self-regulating, collaborative nature of interorganizational networks. Using action research to develop networks also enables members to create real meaning for these general values in particular situations.

Cases covered in this book demonstrate the possibility of developing interorganizational networks to meet varied demands in distinctly different situations. The New Baldwin Corridor Coalition has developed over a five-year period, to help develop a quality industrial community for the twenty-first century. Key stakeholders from the community (business, labor, education, government, community) comprise the coalition. Collaborative work among stakeholders has helped move the community closer to a shared vision of a community for the next century. Work with the CN Incubator Group was designed to create and develop a network organization among 14 independent local business incubators scattered throughout a large region of Pennsylvania. Using an action research process to develop an interorganizational network resulted in making considerable progress in bringing a new network system into being in one year. Developing the Interchurch Network for Social Concerns represents a third use of network concepts. Here, these concepts enabled diverse individuals, groups, and organizations to organize to address larger social issues in a small rural town. The emergent role of INSC has become to identify, define, and develop consensus about broad-based community issues, help focus attention, and provide support by finding effective ways of dealing with them.

Two cases in Chapter 10 suggest other possibilities for developing network organizations to deal with complex, macrolevel issues. The Nordvest Forum has used a strategy of stimulating and supporting learning to improve the managerial capacity in a large region of Norway. This strategy aims to improve the international competitiveness of the region. Several outcomes indicate that the network has made measurable progress toward this goal since 1989.

The Collaborative Alliance for Romanian Orphans case covers a network that developed from dealing with a crisis situation in 1990. Early experience in providing direct assistance led to recognizing a need for strategic intervention. Coming to this realization led to developing a knowledge alliance, Integrative Program Development (IPD). IPD has developed a large interorganizational network of many different types of organizations scattered throughout the world. IPD activity enabled over 125 organizations to collaborate around a shared vision: providing for the overall developmental needs of Romanian children. Outcomes indicate that substantial progress has been made in meeting these needs.

Experience in these few cases merely hints at possible future use of interorganizational networks to address complex "messes" that increasingly confront political leaders, managers, union leaders, community leaders, and ordinary citizens.

Other possible uses of interorganizational networks to deal with complex problems and issues abound. To illustrate, two situations that might benefit from building effective interorganizational networks have become apparent to me in the past month. One deals with getting various stakeholders (federal and state government, business, labor, community residents, environmental groups) involved in inventing ways of protecting the natural environment while fostering sustainable economic development. The second involves developing a statewide nutrition education network that supports collaboration among federal, state, and local programs for low-income families. These two examples only suggest the importance of networks for dealing with multifaceted future problems and issues. Many other possibilities exist.

Working to develop the three interorganizational networks described in Chapters 2 through 8 led to several conclusions:

1. Using network concepts is crucial to the development process.
2. Network members and outsiders often have difficulty understanding networks.
3. Using action research is essential to developing network organizations.
4. Effective design work is essential to the network development process.
5. Developers must be prepared to revise designs based on emerging conditions.
6. Much development work must be integrated with conducting normal network activities.
7. Building and maintaining grassroots support is crucial to network development.

8. Maintaining and developing networks requires creating appropriate forms of organization.
9. The process of developing network organizations is disorderly and nonlinear.
10. It takes a system to change a system.

There are no prescriptions to follow. Rather, insights from these experiences merely give general input for developing other network organizations in different settings. Identified learnings are quite general and, even when applicable, their meaning must be created within the context of specific change efforts. In addition, interorganizational networks are extremely complex and dynamic systems because of their loosely linked, open nature. Consequently, learnings from previous direct network experiences often provide only starting points for working out appropriate ways of dealing with new situations. And benefits from today's learnings may become tomorrow's burden. Hence, maintaining the capacity of network organizations to remain flexible and create new understanding from complex new information and experiences is critical.

While the potential of interorganizational networks is great, they offer no magic solutions. But they do offer representatives of diverse stakeholders a way of organizing to make a difference in many key areas. In addition, the general approach to network development used in cases included in the book suggests ways for OD practitioners to become involved in helping stakeholders create and develop these complex systems. Engaging in interorganizational network development will offer many of us serious challenges and much exciting work for years to come.

Laszlo (1994) briefly describes the future that lies ahead:

> We can now identify the post-modern age with a little more specificity. Ours will be a global society, integrated yet diversified, dynamic and complex, and organized on many levels, from the grass roots to the global. But, we must add, it may or may not come about in reality.
>
> *(Laszlo, 1994, p. 52)*

Our success depends largely on how we conceive of and develop organizational forms that can be effective under the new conditions. Developing interorganizational networks via action research is one key to creating a desirable future.

References

Ackoff, R. R. 1974. *Redesigning the future.* New York: Wiley Interscience.

Alter, C., and J. Hage. 1993. *Organizations working together.* Newbury Park, CA: Sage.

Argyris, C., and D. A. Schon. 1996. *Organizational learning II: Theory, method, and practice.* Reading, MA: Addison-Wesley.

Bell, D. 1976. *The coming of post-industrial society: A venture in social forecasting.* New York: Basic Books.

Bilimoria, D., T. B. Wilmot, and D. L. Cooperrider. 1996. "Multiorganizational and collaboration for global change: New opportunities for organizational change and development." In R. W. Woodman and W. A. Pasmore, eds., *Research in Organizational Change and Development,* Greenwich, CT: JAI Press.

Brown, L. D. 1987. "Development partnerships: Problem-solving at institutional interfaces." Paper presented at the annual meeting of the American Society for Public Administration, Boston.

—— 1993. "Social change through collective reflection with Asian nongovernmental development." *Human Relations,* 46(2), 249–274.

Chisholm, R. F. 1996. "On the meaning of networks." *Group and Organization Management.* 21:2, 216–235.

——1997. "Building a network organization to foster economic development." *International Journal of Public Administration,* 20, 2, 451–477.

Chisholm, R. F., and M. Elden. 1993. "Features of emerging action research." In M. Elden and R. F. Chisholm, eds., *Special issue on action research. Human Relations,* 46(2), 275–297.

Coleman, J. S. 1990. *Foundations of social theory.* Cambridge, Mass.: Harvard University Press.

Cooperrider, D. L., and D. Bilimoria. 1993. "The challenge of global change for strategic management: Opportunities for charting a new course." In P. Shrivasta, A. Huff, and J. Dutton, eds., *Advances in strategic management: Responding to a changing worlds.* vol. 9.

Emery, F. E. 1978. *The fifth Kondradieff wave*. Canberra: Center for Continuing Education, Australian National University.

Emery, M., and F. E. Emery. 1978. "Searching." In J. W. Sutherland (Ed.), *Management handbook of public administration* (pp. 257–301). New York: Van Nostrand Reinhold.

Emery, M. and Purser, R. E. 1996. *The Search Conference: A Powerful Way for Planning Organization Change and Community Action*. San Francisco: Jossey-Bass.

Finsrud, H. 1995. How about a dialogue? Communication perspective meets socioecological perspective. In O. Eikeland and H. D. Finsrud, eds., Oslo: Work Research Institute.

Gricar, B. G., and L. D. Brown. 1981. "Conflict, power and organization in a changing community." *Human Relations*, 34(10), 877–893.

Gustavsen, B. 1992. *Dialogue and development*. Assen/Maastricht, Netherlands: Van Gorcum.

Hage, J., and C. H. Powers. 1992. *Post-industrial lives*. Newbury Park, CA: Sage.

Hanssen-Bauer, J., and C. C. Snow. 1996. "Responding to hypercompetition: The structure and processes of a regional learning network organization." *Organization Science*, 7:4, 413–427.

Herbst, P. G. 1976. *Alternatives to hierarchies*. Leiden, Netherlands: Nijoff.

Kanter, R. M. 1995. *World class*. New York: Simon and Schuster.

Knoke, W. 1996. *Bold new world*. New York: Kodansha International.

Laszlo, E. 1994. *Vision 2020: Reordering chaos for global survival*. Langhorne, PA: Gordon and Breach.

Lewin, K. 1946. Action research and minority problems. *Journal of Social Issues,* 2:4, 34–46.

Pasmore, W. A. 1988. *Designing effective organizations: The sociotechnical systems perspective*. New York: Wiley.

Perlmutter, H., and E. L. Trist. 1986. "Paradigms for social transition." *Human Relations*, 39:1, 1–27.

Senge, P. M. 1990. "The leader's new work: building learning organizations." *Sloan Management Review*, 32:1, 19–35.

Susman, G. I. and R. Evered. 1978. An assessment of the scientific merit of action research. *Administrative Science Quarterly*, 23, 582–603.

Sweeney, C., and A. Brandon. 1996. "The flight." *New York Times Magazine*, September 29, 1996, 108-109.

Trist, E. L. 1983. "Referent organizations and the development of interorganizational domains." *Human Relations*, 36(3), 269–284.

———— 1985. "Intervention strategies for interorganizational domains." In R. Tannenbaum and F. Massarik, eds., *Human systems development: New perspectives on people and organizations*. San Francisco: Jossey-Bass.

————1986. "Quality of working life and community development: Some reflections on the Jamestown experience." *Journal of Applied Behavioral Science*, 22(3), 223–238.

Weick, K. E. 1979. *The social psychology of organizing*. Reading, MA: Addison-Wesley.

————1989. "Theory construction as disciplined imagination, *Academy of Management Review*, 14(4), 516–531.

Weisbord, M. R. 1992. *Discovering common ground*. San Francisco: Berrett-Koehler.

Name Index

Subject Index